Praise for *Umbrella G*  *houses:*

"This new edition of the N(ashington
lighthouses . . . is an important addition to the libraries of lighthouse
enthusiasts, and a must for those visiting the lighthouses of the
Evergreen State."

> Wayne C. Wheeler, President
> United States Lighthouse Society

"This second edition of the *Umbrella Guide to Washington Lighthouses*
is full of fresh, new anecdotes about the lights and their keepers. It
makes you want to visit each lighthouse and feel the history of it."

> Captain E. L. Davis, Director
> Coast Guard Museum Northwest

"This book will add to the enjoyment of those who visit or stay for a
week at our lighthouse."

> Eric Henriksson
> New Dungeness Chapter
> United States Lighthouse Society

"Both historians and travelers will welcome this fascinating new look
at Washington's lighthouses. The details about the building of each
light and the technical information about the equipment are perfectly
melded with the stories of the keepers, their families, and their lifestyles.
The authors also let you know which lighthouses welcome visitors,
and include the necessary specifics. Well done."

> Ken Black, Director
> Shoreline Museum
> Maine's Lighthouse Museum

"A concise and informative addition to the recorded history of
Northwest lighthouses."

> Mavis Stears
> Points Northeast Historical Society

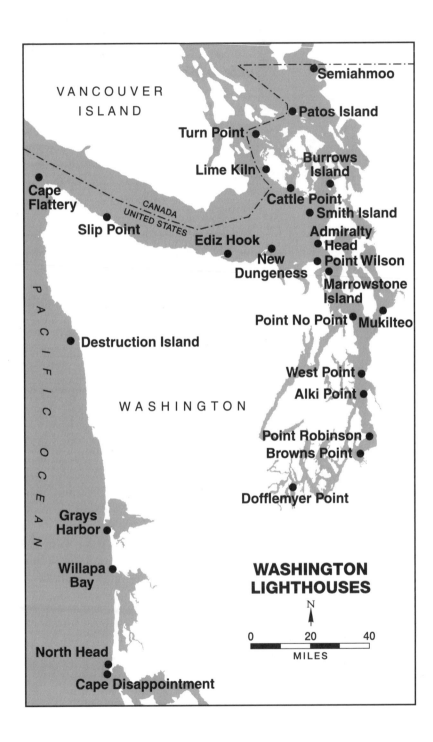

VANCOUVER
ISLAND

Semiahmoo

Patos Island

Turn Point

Burrows
Island

Lime Kiln

Cattle Point

Cape
Flattery

CANADA
UNITED STATES

Smith Island

Slip Point

Admiralty
Head

Ediz Hook

Point Wilson

New
Dungeness

Marrowstone
Island

PACIFIC

Point No Point Mukilteo

Destruction Island

West Point

WASHINGTON

Alki Point

Point Robinson

OCEAN

Browns Point

Dofflemyer Point

Grays
Harbor

Willapa
Bay

**WASHINGTON
LIGHTHOUSES**

N

0   20   40

North Head

MILES

Cape Disappointment

Umbrella Guide to
Washington Lighthouses

by Sharlene and Ted Nelson

Updated 2nd Edition

UMBRELLA
BOOKS

Published by Epicenter Press, Inc.

Umbrella Books™ are a series of regional travel guides focusing on destinations in Alaska, Washington, Oregon, and California.

Editor: Christine Ummel
Cover design: Elizabeth Watson
Front cover photo: The Mukilteo Lighthouse at sunset. Photo by John McAnulty.
Back cover photos: Top: The North Head Lighthouse near Cape Disappointment. Photo by Ted Nelson. Middle: The Cape Disappointment Lighthouse's fourth-order Fresnel lens. Photo by Ted Nelson. Bottom: The Point Robinson Lighthouse between Seattle and Tacoma. Photo by Ted Nelson.
Maps: Rusty Nelson
Inside design: Sue Mattson
Printer: Best Book Manufacturers

Text ©1998 Sharlene and Ted Nelson
ISBN 0-945397-70-4
Library of Congress Catalog Card Number: 98-073058

To order single copies of UMBRELLA GUIDE TO WASHINGTON LIGHTHOUSES, mail $12.95 (Washington residents add $1.11 state sales tax) plus $3 for shipping and handling to: Epicenter Press, Box 82368, Kenmore, WA 98028. BOOKSELLERS: Retail discounts are available from major wholesalers.

PRINTED IN CANADA
First Printing August 1998
10 9 8 7 6 5 4 3 2 1

Contents

Foreword

This is a new edition of the Nelsons' definitive book about Washington lighthouses. The first edition, published in 1990, became one in a trilogy of books about West Coast lighthouses.

Much has changed at Washington's lighthouses since 1990. The U.S. Coast Guard still maintains the automated lights and fog signals, but resident Coast Guard keepers no longer live at the stations. Under lease or transfer agreements with the Coast Guard, many of the lighthouses and even some of the original keepers' dwellings are becoming accessible to the public.

In this new edition, the Nelsons describe these changes. They also have woven previously unpublished information into the rich human history of the state's lighthouses. As before, they tell the stories of the lightships and lighthouse tenders, and the lenses, lights, and fog signals that have served Washington's mariners for over a century.

Historic and current photographs complement the narrative, and maps show how to reach the lighthouses. The Nelsons also tell how to visit the stations, even how to stay in some old keepers' dwellings where lodging is available.

This new book is an important addition to the libraries of lighthouse enthusiasts, and a must for those visiting the lighthouses of the Evergreen State.

Wayne C. Wheeler, President
United States Lighthouse Society

Acknowledgments

We thank all who helped us with the two editions of this book. From the beginning, Gene Davis, curator of the Coast Guard Museum Northwest, and assistants Larry Dubia and D. A. Webb shared their knowledge, research materials, and photos.

Coast Guard personnel who gave freely of their time include Michael Pierson and staff at Port Angeles; Pam Russell, and Charles Tanzki and staff at Seattle; and Andrew Walker at Astoria.

Insights about lighthouse life came from Helga and Charles Settles, Dorothy Zauner Armstrong, and historians Etta Egeland and Murrial Short.

We were also assisted by personnel at the National Archives and others at museums, libraries, and historical societies, including Donna Cloud, Shirley Dinsmore, Christine Harris, William Hanable, and Eric Henriksson. Information about parks came from Debra Brown, Larry Chapman, Melanie Ford, Barbara Kachel, Evan Roberts, Albert Shepard, and Linda Versage.

Books by Archie Binns, Harriet Fish, Helene Glidden, James Gibbs, and Mavis Stears were valuable resources for us.

We thank, too, Wayne C. Wheeler and the staff of the U.S. Lighthouse Society, and Rusty Nelson, who created our maps. We owe special thanks to all those whose quotes within the narrative helped make our stories complete.

Lastly, we thank the late Jerry Miller, who published the first edition, and Kent Sturgis and Christine Ummel at Epicenter Press, who made this second edition a reality.

Introduction

Washington was a territory when its first lighthouse was completed on Cape Disappointment, at the mouth of the Columbia River, in 1856. The original tower still stands, and its light still shines out to sea and across the river's treacherous bar.

Then, even more than now, Washington depended on maritime trade. Its waters were its highways. Lights, fog signals, and lightships were needed to guide mariners along the coast, through the Strait of Juan de Fuca, and along inland waters.

Twenty-six lighthouse stations were built on Washington's shores, most tended by resident keepers and their families. Lightships were anchored at three offshore locations. The lighthouse stations and lightships were supplied by lighthouse tenders. These lights and the men and women who tended them played important roles in Washington's history.

These aids to mariners had their genesis in the nation's first public works act, passed by Congress in 1789. It provided for lighthouses along U.S. waters, "for rendering the navigation thereof easy and safe." The Lighthouse Establishment created under the act was first administered by the Treasury Department, and for a time it was under the personal supervision of Alexander Hamilton.

An inquiry in 1851, however, determined that the U.S. lighthouse system had become far less effective than those of other maritime nations. In response, Congress created the Lighthouse Board that would manage the Lighthouse Service for fifty-eight years. One of the board's first acts was to adopt the French-designed Fresnel lens for use in all U.S. lighthouses.

The Lighthouse Board was abolished in 1910, and the Lighthouse Service became a bureau of the Department of Commerce. In 1939, at the urging of President Franklin D. Roosevelt, management of the lighthouses, lightships, and tenders was transferred to the U.S. Coast Guard.

COAST GUARD MUSEUM NORTHWEST

Prior to 1914, the light at Point Wilson shone from a tower atop the keepers' dwelling, which still stands today.

The Coast Guard began automating the lights and fog signals in the 1960s, and gradually the resident keepers left the lighthouses. Lightships were retired and replaced by automated buoys. Today Washington's coastal lights and fog signals are maintained by the Coast Guard's Aids to Navigation Team Astoria, Oregon; lights and fog signals on inland waters are maintained by the Aids to Navigation Team Puget Sound, stationed in Seattle.

Even after automation, much remains of the state's lighthouse history. Many of the original lighthouses stand, and some still use a Fresnel lens. The Coast Guard has made stations available to groups or agencies that maintain and care for them. At these stations, visitors can climb the tower stairs as the first lightkeepers did, and at some, the keepers' residences are available for lodging.

This guide describes such opportunities and tells the history of Washington's twenty-six lighthouses, its lightships and lighthouse tenders, and the men and women who made sure that "the light shall not fail."

9

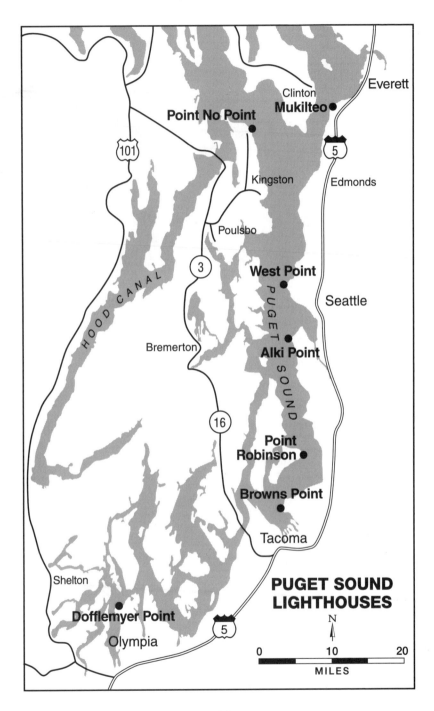

Clinton
Everett
Mukilteo
Point No Point
101
5
Kingston
Edmonds
Poulsbo
3
West Point
Seattle
HOOD CANAL
Bremerton
Alki Point
PUGET SOUND
16
Point Robinson
Browns Point
Tacoma
Shelton
PUGET SOUND LIGHTHOUSES
Dofflemyer Point
N
5
Olympia
0   10   20
MILES

PUGET SOUND PROTECTORS

Puget Sound was discovered by British explorer Captain George Vancouver in 1792. He explored the northern sound, then dispatched Lieutenant Peter Puget to explore the lower reaches in two small boats. It took the Puget party six days to reach the sound's southern end. Vancouver named the sound in Puget's honor.

The sound's main channel is generally broad with a narrow passage at the Tacoma Narrows. Depths range to 600 feet. For mariners, the sound presents a series of points and bays that are useful for navigation on days with good visibility, but the many points become hazards at night and in fog.

The sound's lighthouses and fog signals were built in response to the growth of the region's maritime trade. At first lumber was shipped to California, then to Hawaii and Asia, and coal was shipped to San Francisco. Later, inbound vessels brought rails for the transcontinental railroads and finished goods from the East Coast.

Completion of the railroads spurred the shipment of eastern Washington's grain and flour to world markets. Then the waters were heavily trafficked by small steamers, called the "Mosquito Fleet," that carried passengers and freight between Puget Sound communities.

Seven lighthouses were built along the sound, and all remain today: Mukilteo, West Point, Alki Point, and Browns Point on the east side; Point No Point and Point Robinson on the west side; and Dofflemyer Point near Olympia.

Visitors to the Mukilteo Lighthouse, built in 1906, can take tours of the station and see its Fresnel lens still in use.

1. Mukilteo Lighthouse

On March 2, 1906, the *Everett Morning Tribune* reported in bold headlines: "Lamp Lit in New Mukilteo Tower . . . Best Light House in Entire Puget Sound District." The *Tribune* reporter wrote excitedly, "last night . . . dozens of people curiously watched the glimmer of the lamp as it shot its beam of yellow light in the direction of the city at regular intervals."

Some fifty years earlier, in January 1855, Isaac Stevens, the Governor of Washington Territory, had met with Native Americans at Muckl-te-oh to sign a treaty with leaders of twenty tribes. The town later founded here was originally called Point Elliot. In 1862, however, store owner J. D. Fowler became the town's postmaster and changed its name back to Mukilteo, which means "good camping ground."

Although Point Elliot (called Elliot Point on modern charts) did not present a hazard like other lighthouse sites, the Lighthouse Board in 1901 decided that "a light and fog signal would be of much benefit to navigation." Large vessels turned at the point on their way to Everett's harbor, while others traveled up Possession Sound and Saratoga Passage, "which route is much frequented by the smaller boats running out of Tacoma and Seattle."

Construction of the station began in 1905, and when completed it consisted of two keepers' dwellings and a thirty-eight-foot-high octagonal tower attached to a fog signal building. Compressors on the building's main floor powered a Daboll trumpet.

The light source for the fourth-order Fresnel lens, according to the *Tribune* account, was "nothing more than a small circular burner, similar to an ordinary Rochester parlor lamp." The reporter described the two keepers' dwellings as modern in every respect — equipped with steam heat, baths, and everything to be found in any up-to-date house. Next to one dwelling stood a windmill to pump water from a well.

The *Tribune* also noted that the appointment of Peter N. Christiansen as principal keeper "comes as a reward for his faithful services." The reporter concluded that "the light station is open to visitors at all times, who will find Keeper Christianson [*sic*] both hospitable and entertaining."

Christiansen was born in Norway and went to sea at age fourteen. He served in the Merchant Marine for eleven years and in the United States Navy for ten years, then joined the Lighthouse Service. In 1893, he became the first assistant keeper at Turn Point Lighthouse. While there, he and principal keeper Edward Durgan rescued men from the vessel *Enterprise* caught in a severe February storm in 1897. Both received certificates of merit for their heroic efforts.

Christiansen's assistant at Mulkilteo was O. Kinyon, who had transferred from Destruction Island Lighthouse where he had served three years. Like other keepers, Christiansen and Kinyon tended the light as instructed by an 1871 manual: "Every evening, half an hour before sunset, the keepers provided with a lighting lamp, will ascend the tower and commence lighting the lamp . . . so that the light may have its full effect by the time twilight ends."

After thirty-one years with the Lighthouse Service, Christiansen died in 1925 while at the Mukilteo Lighthouse. His wife served as keeper until Edward A. Brooks took over. While Brooks was keeper in 1927, electricity was installed at the station, and the kerosene lamp was replaced by a Thomas Edison bulb, the largest and brightest bulb then available.

Brooks was replaced by Ray Dunson in 1937. Dunson, who had earlier served at Smith Island, stayed at Mukilteo until 1939, when the Coast Guard took over the station. In the 1960s, the Coast

Guard planned to replace the Fresnel lens with a modern optic. Residents of Everett and Mukilteo protested, however, and the Fresnel lens stayed. It and a modern fog signal were automated in 1979.

One of the last coast guardsmen to serve as resident keeper at the station was Kurtis Betz from Winnemucca, Nevada. Between 1986 and 1990, he maintained the grounds and the lighthouse, and gave tours. Betz became interested in the station's history and collected artifacts from its past, some of which can be seen in the fog signal room. The displays include copies of the 1855 treaty, Christiansen's certificate of merit, and the recently acquired Fresnel lens from Oregon's Desdemona Sands Lighthouse.

In 1991 the Coast Guard leased the lighthouse — which by then was on the National Register of Historic Sites — to the city of Mukilteo. The two keepers' dwellings were leased to the city in 1996.

Today the Mukilteo Historical Society cares for the station. Volunteers Mim Loree and Chris Wilson enthusiastically described the society's plans: With help from the Boeing Company, one of the keepers' dwellings will be restored and furnished to its early 1900s style. The second dwelling will accommodate lodgers, who will assist other volunteers in conducting lighthouse tours. When these restorations are complete, the station will be much as it was when the *Tribune* called it "the Best Light on the Sound."

Directions and Hours:

Follow signs to Mukilteo and the Mukilteo ferry from I-5 Exit 189. The lighthouse is next to the ferry dock. Both the lighthouse and fog signal room are open April through Labor Day, Saturdays, Sundays, and holidays, noon-5. For current information, call the city of Mukilteo at (425) 355-4141.

Puget Sound's first lighthouse was built on Point No Point and began operation in 1880 with a kerosene lantern.

2. Point No Point Lighthouse

The oldest lighthouse on Puget Sound, the Point No Point Lighthouse, was completed in 1880. It stands on the west side, near where Admiralty Inlet ends and the sound begins. The point's name was given by Lieutenant Charles Wilkes of the Wilkes Expedition in 1841. From his ship, Wilkes saw what appeared to be a low point of land extending far into the sound. As he sailed closer, it proved to be less prominent than expected, so he named it Point No Point. Native Americans called it Hahd-skus, or "long nose."

At this point fourteen years later, Isaac Stevens, the first Governor of Washington Territory, met with one thousand Native Americans who lived between the Olympic Mountains' crest and Puget Sound to sign a treaty. A bronze plaque commemorating the event is near the lighthouse.

By the late 1860s, lighthouses had been guiding mariners along the Washington coast and the Strait of Juan de Fuca for over a decade, but there were no lights south of Admiralty Head. At night and in fog, ships' captains navigated by dead reckoning or anchored until skies cleared. One captain, on the bark *Iconium*, didn't wait for the fog to lift. He ran his ship aground on this isolated point in 1868.

Puget Sound maritime traffic was expected to increase when the Northern Pacific Railroad reached Tacoma, and the Lighthouse Board reported that this increase "require[d] the construction of such aids to navigation as will effectually open these waters to foreign as well as home trade." So in 1872 the board requested $25,000 to build a lighthouse on Point No Point.

Even though the board received the money the following year, construction was delayed by disagreement about the best location. The board wanted the lighthouse on Point No Point, but local Lighthouse Service officials wanted it farther north on Foulweather Bluff. When they agreed on Point No Point, the landowners, Francis and Mary Anne James, were reluctant to sell. Mr. James, a councilman and store owner in Port Townsend, wanted an "exorbitant price," according to the board.

Settling on a price proved difficult, perhaps because of a bad experience in Mr. James's past. Thirteen years earlier, he had served briefly as principal keeper at Cape Flattery. His temper had caused a gun duel there, but no one was hurt.

After four years of negotiations, a price was agreed on. The Jameses sold forty acres to the Lighthouse Service for $1,000 in April 1879, and construction of the lighthouse finally began.

When principal keeper J. S. Maggs, a dentist from Seattle, and his assistant Henry H. Edwards arrived at the point in late December, the buildings were not completed, and neither the lens nor the glass for the lantern had been delivered. But Maggs was determined to show a light. First he hung canvas over the south window openings in the lantern room to keep out the cold wind. Then he hung a household kerosene lantern in the tower, and lit it on January 1, 1880.

The following days were no less frantic. At night Maggs and Edwards fought wind, snow, and cold to keep the lantern lit. During the day, they helped prepare the incomplete dwelling for the arrival of Maggs's pregnant wife.

She came in February, the same month that the lantern glass and fifth-order Fresnel lens were installed. A fog bell, formerly used at the New Dungeness Lighthouse, was in place by April, and the station passed inspection.

To make the keepers' life a bit easier, the Lighthouse Service cut a horseback trail through dense brush to the sawmill town of Port Gamble, a few miles to the west. The keepers could use this

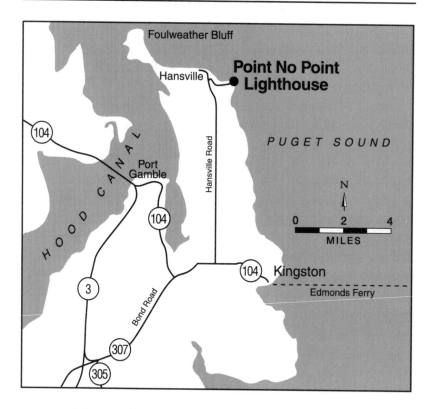

route to pick up mail instead of rowing the nine miles to Port Ludlow over water that, according to the board, was "sometimes dangerous to cross in a small boat."

The station's supplies came by boat. Shortly before the Maggses' baby girl was born in July, Mr. Maggs bought a cow. It was delivered on a schooner, lowered over the ship's side in a sling, and swam ashore.

Maggs and his family left Point No Point in 1884, and he was replaced by W. H. Jankins. Four years later, Irish-born Edward Scannell replaced Jankins, beginning nearly a half century when only two principal keepers served at Point No Point.

Many changes took place during those fifty years. In 1900 the fog bell was replaced by a Daboll trumpet. The compressor for the fog signal was run by a kerosene engine. In 1915 the lens was changed to a larger fourth-order Fresnel lens, which is still in use despite a cracked prism, damaged when the tower was struck by lightning in 1931.

For forty years no roads reached Point No Point. Except for mail from Port Gamble, everything and everyone came and left by boat. Nevertheless, a few loggers and fishermen built houses along the beach north of the station, which soon became a center for the scattered settlement.

The first schoolhouse was built nearby. In 1893 the Point No Point Post Office opened, and Mrs. Scannell, the keeper's wife, became the postmistress. When the Scannells left in 1914, assistant W. H. Cary took over as principal keeper, and the post office was moved to nearby Hansville.

For a time, Cary's wife owned and ran a store in Hansville. Then in the 1930s she became a weather reporter. A weather vane and an anemometer were mounted on the dwelling's roof and connected to an instrument panel in the sitting room. Three times a day, Mrs. Cary took readings from the panel and phoned the information to the weather bureau at Boeing Field in Seattle.

The Carys left in 1937, but weather reporting remained a duty for the coast guardsmen who followed them. After the station was automated in 1977, only one man was assigned there at a time. James Teeter was one of the last coast guardsman to care for the light. Besides relaying weather reports to the National Oceanic and Atmospheric Administration in Seattle, he mowed the lawn, conducted tours, painted buildings, and once he rescued boaters.

During a snowstorm, a small boat carrying three people lost power and drifted toward Point No Point. In the twilight and cold, Teeter saw the boat. "I'll wade out for them, but I won't swim," he said. As the boat came closer, Teeter waded into the frigid water and pulled the boat and its frightened passengers to shore. It was too late for them to catch the next ferry to Seattle, so Teeter made them comfortable for the night in the keepers' dwelling.

The last coast guardsmen at the station were assigned to the icebreaker *Polar Sea*. They left in 1997, and the dwelling stood empty.

Directions and Hours

In the summer of 1998 the Coast Guard was concluding negotiations to lease the station to the Kitsap County Fair and Parks Department. The department plans to make the station accessible and to offer tours. For current information, call the Kitsap County Fair and Parks Department at (360) 895-3895.

The West Point Lighthouse, which marks the northern entrance to Elliott Bay, can be seen in Seattle's Discovery Park.

3. West Point Lighthouse

Established in 1881, the West Point Lighthouse, at the foot of Seattle's Magnolia Bluff in Discovery Park, stands at one of the busiest vessel traffic intersections in Washington waters. Freighters, tugs, and pleasure boats stream by between ports north and south and into Seattle's Elliott Bay. Just north of the lighthouse, boats sail in and out of the Lake Washington Ship Canal, which connects Puget Sound with Lake Union and Lake Washington.

West Point was quiet and remote in 1872, when the Lighthouse Board recommended a light be established here and at Point No Point. The recommendation was made in anticipation of the Northern Pacific Railroad's arrival in Tacoma the following year.

By 1879 work was proceeding on the Point No Point Lighthouse, but no appropriation had been made for West Point. That year the board repeated its request for funding for West Point, but this time for only a fog signal: "It is highly essential that this magnificent sheet of water, which has not its equal in the world, should be so marked by fog signals as to render its navigation from Cape Flattery to Olympia possible at all times without danger to life and property."

But once again the board's plans changed. By 1881 funds were appropriated to build both a light and fog signal at the point, which the board described as "the first prominent sand spit north of the busy town of Seattle."

In October principal keeper A. W. Martin and assistant A. Prusham moved into the station's dwelling. They lit the lamp inside a fourth-order Fresnel lens on November 15, 1881. The square brick tower, on the end of the spit, stood twenty-seven feet high. Behind the lighthouse, from a small frame tower, hung the fog bell, which had previously been used at Cape Disappointment.

Two years later George F. Fonda was appointed keeper, but he served alone; assistant keeper positions at several Washington lighthouses had been eliminated to reduce costs. But a new barn stood at the station, and Fonda could ride a horse on a freshly blazed trail that led up the bluff to a county road leading to Seattle.

Soon after Fonda arrived, he and all lightkeepers were issued their first uniforms: navy blue trousers, a matching double-breasted coat with brass buttons, and a billed cap. The Lighthouse Board reported that it had "at last succeeded in clothing all the male lightkeepers and officers and crews of lightships and lighthouse tenders in a neat, appropriate, and economical uniform."

Fonda finally got an assistant in 1886, when a Daboll trumpet replaced the station's fog bell. A new building housed the trumpet's coal-fired engines, and an assistant keeper's dwelling was built. The new fog signal began operation in February 7, 1887 and lasted until its engines wore out in 1901. The following year a replacement fog signal, with oil-fired engines, was installed in a building added to the tower's west side.

During Fonda's time the station was frequently endangered by winter storms that eroded the spit. After each storm, the breakwater and dikes were reinforced with logs, planks, brush, and gravel. In 1891 the board reported the positioning of 250 cubic yards of stone "which it is hoped will permanently protect the point."

The station became less remote at the turn of the century when army troops moved into the new Fort Lawton on Magnolia Bluff. Completion of the Lake Washington Ship Canal in 1915 brought more vessel traffic past the point. While coast guardsmen tended the light in 1966, the West Point Sewage Treatment Plant was built east of the station.

Thirteen years later the West Point Lighthouse was scheduled for automation. The keeper, First Class Boswain's Mate Marvin

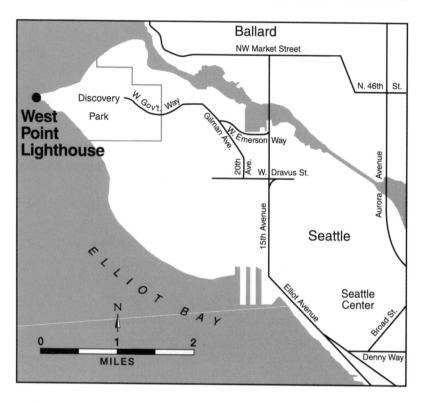

Gerbers, told a newspaper reporter, "It would be nice if they kept it open at least until November 15 [1981] . . . when it is 100." Gerbers didn't look forward to moving his wife and two children away from the lighthouse home the family had come to love. Gerbers was even used to the foghorn. When talking to someone while the signal was on, he would stop speaking every twenty-seven seconds during the blast, then resume talking.

A lack of funds delayed the automation date, so Gerbers got his wish. On the lighthouse's one hundredth birthday, in a show of appreciation and celebration, Gerbers climbed up on the roof and poured a bottle of champagne over the lighthouse.

In February 1985 the station became the last in Washington to be automated. Today its Fresnel lens, flashing red and white, rotates twenty-four hours a day, and its modern fog signal is activated by an electric sensor. The two keepers' dwellings became family residences for Coast Guard personnel stationed in Seattle.

Directions and Hours:

The station is fenced and closed to the public, but the light-house can be seen from the beach. Access is through Discovery Park by walking 1.5 miles or bicycling on paved surfaces. The road to the station is restricted to authorized vehicles only.

Limited vehicle beach parking permits are available at Discovery Park Visitor Center on a first-come, first-served basis to the disabled, to seniors over 62 years old, to families with children five years and under, or to educational groups. Inquire at the visitor center about weekend summertime shuttles to the beach.

The visitor center is open daily 8:30-5 except holidays. The park is open 6 a.m.-11 p.m. Phone (206) 386-4236.

4. Alki Point Lighthouse

The Alki Point Lighthouse in West Seattle marks the southern entrance to Seattle's harbor, Elliott Bay. Since the station was built in 1913, homes and condominiums have crowded close to its small, pie-shaped reservation.

The Denny party of Seattle pioneers landed on this point in 1851, optimistically naming their anticipated settlement New York. Growth progressed slowly, and "Alki," a Chinook Indian word for "by and by," was added, so the name became New York-Alki. Later, the United States Coast Survey named the point Battery Point, but the name Alki prevailed.

According to traditional stories, Hans Martin Hanson provided the point's first light. In 1868 he and his brother-in-law bought 320 acres there for $450 and built a home where they, their wives, and seven children lived. Concerned about the safety of ships sailing by, Hanson set a lantern on the beach each night.

The first official light was a post light — a lens lantern hung on a wooden scaffold — established by the Lighthouse Service in 1887. Hanson was hired to tend the light for $15 a month. Twice a year a lighthouse tender unloaded barrels of fuel on the beach. Since Hanson lived close by, he lit the light each evening and extinguished it in the morning. Post lights elsewhere were left burning continuously and refueled weekly.

Tending the light soon became a family affair. Hanson's son Edmund, the only boy of the seven children in the household, sometimes assumed this duty. When he didn't want to walk the planks across the tide flats to the light, he cajoled one of his sisters or his cousins into tending it.

TED NELSON

The Alki Point Lighthouse, built in 1913, was a great improvement over the previous light, a lens lantern on a post.

In 1895 the Lighthouse Service recognized that the point's post light was of little value in thick fog, and recommended "that a fog bell with suitable dwelling, grounds etc. could be erected for $6000." Seven years later appropriations were made, but difficulties arose.

Before the elder Hanson died, he had divided his property among his children. His son Edmund became the owner of the parcel that the Lighthouse Service wanted. Edmund's uncle, Ivar Haglund, owner of Seattle's famous restaurant Ivar's Acres of Clams, described Edmund as a flamboyant man. He often dressed in a striped coat, gray trousers, and fancy shirts, accented with yellow gloves and a derby hat. Yet despite his flashy style, Edmund was a tough negotiator. He refused to sell for the price offered.

Eventually more appropriations were made, and Edmund sold the property for $9,000. On June 1, 1913, the Alki Point Lighthouse Station finally went into operation at a cost of $47,000 — almost eight times the original estimate.

The fog signal building, with compressors that powered a Daboll trumpet, stood near the beach. Attached was a thirty-seven-foot-high tower with an incandescent oil-vapor lamp that provided light for a fourth-order Fresnel lens. Two dwellings for the keepers stood behind the lighthouse. Inside the fog signal building, the lens lantern that the Hanson family tended for twenty-six years was placed on display.

Albert G. Anderson became Alki's principal keeper in 1950. Destined to be one of the last civilian keepers on the West Coast, Anderson had joined the Lighthouse Service in 1927, first serving on the Columbia River Lightship, then on the lighthouse tender *Rose*. In 1939 he was assigned to Oregon's Cape Blanco Lighthouse, where he served until moving to Alki Point. Unlike other lighthouse keepers who joined the Coast Guard when it took over the lighthouses, Anderson chose to remain a civilian.

While Anderson was on duty at Alki Point in the 1960s, a modern optic replaced the fourth-order Fresnel lens. The lens was taken to the Admiralty Head Lighthouse Museum in Fort Casey State Park, where it is still on display.

Anderson retired in 1970. That same year the old lens lantern tended by the Hansons was stolen from the lighthouse. A few years later, a woman from southern California asked a Seattle antique dealer about its value. Her husband, by then deceased, had bought it at an antique store in Long Beach, California. When told that the lantern had been stolen, the woman returned it to the Coast Guard.

Ironically, the lantern had not been polished, and the thief's fingerprints, still on the brass, led to

TED NELSON

The lens lantern used at Alki Point is now at Seattle's Coast Guard Museum Northwest.

____

his arrest. "He got two years, and we got our lantern," said retired Coast Guard Captain Gene Davis, curator of the Coast Guard Museum Northwest in Seattle, where the lantern is now displayed.

Alki's light and fog signal were automated in 1984. For a time, a resident Coast Guard keeper lived in one of the original dwellings, and the admiral in charge of the Coast Guard's 13th District lived in the other. Now the dwellings are occupied by the commander of Coast Guard Group Seattle and the group's marine safety officer.

The Coast Guard does not intend to lease this station, but volunteers from the Coast Guard Auxiliary conduct tours of the lighthouse. The grounds are available for weddings, in a setting that keeper Anderson once described as having a "million dollar view."

Directions and Hours:

Take Exit 163 off I-5 onto the West Seattle Freeway. At SW Admiral Way turn right and follow Admiral Way to 63rd Avenue SW. Turn right on 63rd to Alki Avenue SW. Turn left on Alki Avenue and follow it to the lighthouse.

The lighthouse is open May-Sept., Sat. and Sun. and most holidays, 12-4. Group tours (ten or more) are by advance appointment, Wed. 11-2. For information, phone the U.S. Coast Guard (206) 217-6123.

The lens lantern is at the Coast Guard Museum Northwest in Seattle on Pier 36, at 1519 Alaskan Way S. Open Mon., Wed., and Fri., 9-3, and Sat. and Sun., 1-5. Phone (206) 217-6993.

Originally just a fog signal station, Point Robinson now has a thirty-eight-foot tower with a rotating Fresnel lens.

5. Point Robinson Lighthouse

Point Robinson, on the northeast corner of Maury Island, is a turning point for vessels sailing between Seattle and Tacoma. Its lighthouse stands on a sandy beach backed by tree-studded bluffs and is often shrouded in fog. Unlike other lighthouse stations in Washington, the one at Point Robinson (also known as Robinson Point) began as a fog signal station.

In early 1884 the Lighthouse Service purchased twenty-four acres on this point. The lighthouse tender *Shubrick* unloaded a work crew in June, along with building materials, fog signal machinery, and a boiler. The boiler and the twelve-inch steam whistle previously had been used at Oregon's Point Adams Lighthouse, near the mouth of the Columbia River.

Unable to finish during the summer, the crew left and returned in March 1885. Two months later a wooden boiler house with the steam whistle projecting from the roof and two cisterns to collect water were completed. They were located near where the present lighthouse stands. A dwelling with green shutters was built one hundred yards away, next to the beach. The station was dedicated on July 1, 1885.

Its first keeper was Franklin Tucker. Age fifty-eight, a seasoned mariner and lighthouse keeper, Tucker had arrived from Cape Flattery. In the 1850s he captained a schooner carrying mail between Olympia, Washington Territory, and Victoria, British Columbia.

He left the ship for lighthouse duty in 1857 when he served as a temporary keeper at the New Dungeness Lighthouse. The collector of customs, however, questioned Tucker's competency as a keeper. "He [Tucker] promised to leave off drinking and lead a sober life, which he has not done," wrote the collector. Nonetheless, Tucker took a lighthouse assignment at Cape Flattery and a second one at New Dungeness. In 1887 he left Point Robinson to serve at Ediz Hook Lighthouse, where he remained for nine years, finally retiring at age seventy — the mandatory retirement age for lighthouse keepers.

The year that Tucker left Point Robinson, a lens lantern showing red was installed near the point's fog signal building. Although it was hung on a twenty-five-foot post, captains soon complained that the light was partially obscured by the dwelling when they were coming from the south. In 1894 an open wooden tower was built, raising the light to thirty-one feet.

For many years one keeper tended the light and fog signal at Point Robinson. In 1897, when the steam whistle blew for 528 hours and the keeper shoveled thirty-five tons of coal, it became evident another keeper was needed. The board requested funds for an assistant keeper and a second dwelling. By 1903 an assistant keeper had arrived, but the second dwelling was not built until 1907.

As maritime traffic continued to grow on Puget Sound, the point's light and fog signal increasingly needed to be improved. In 1915 the present lighthouse, a small fog signal building with an attached tower, was built. Compressors for a new foghorn were installed on the main floor; clockwork machinery was installed in the thirty-eight-foot tower to rotate a fifth-order Fresnel lens. An incandescent oil vapor lamp provided light visible for twelve miles. Partway up the tower's spiral staircase, a door opened into an attic room where the keeper could stay during his watch.

Jens O. Pedersen was assigned keeper at Point Robinson in 1936. He had been with the Lighthouse Service for ten years, serving at Oregon's Tillamook Rock Lighthouse and Washington's Destruction Island. Pedersen remained at Point Robinson when the Coast Guard assumed responsibilities in 1939, and he retired from the point in 1954.

Point Robinson's steam fog signal, lens lantern on a high wooden scaffold, and keepers' dwelling (background), circa 1895.

Coast guardsmen continued the duties of earlier keepers until the light and fog signal were automated in 1978. Then the staff was reduced, leaving only one coast guardsman at Point Robinson. In 1989 Jerry Belstad occupied one of the dwellings with his wife and infant son.

Belstad painted the buildings, maintained the grounds, and conducted tours. In the fog signal room he displayed a guest book first signed in 1893 by a visitor from Mare Island, California.

When Belstad took visitors into the tower, he showed them the original fifth-order Fresnel lens that turns twenty-four hours a day, and the bare curtain rods attached to the lantern walls. Before automation, the light was turned off during the day, and the lens was immobile. Then curtains were drawn around the lens to protect the glass from the sun's rays.

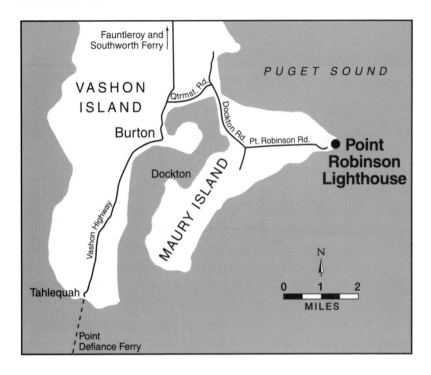

Belstad was one of the last coast guardsmen to serve at Point Robinson. Before leaving, he said that he would never forget the way that on the point it "rains sideways, [nor the] tides that brought the sound right up to the porch. . . . "

The Coast Guard has leased the Point Robinson station to the Vashon Parks District. In 1998, island residents began to develop a long-range plan for the station's use.

Directions and Hours:

Until plans are completed, the station's grounds can be visited by taking a short trail from a parking area on the bluff above. For current information, call the Vashon Parks District at (206) 463-9602.

6. Browns Point Lighthouse

On December 12, 1887, the Lighthouse Service lit a post light on the beach at Browns Point. Two other post lights, one at Point Robinson and one at Alki Point, were lit the same day.

At the time Browns Point (then called Point Brown) and the hills above it were covered with scattered trees and berry vines. Puyallup Indians came here in the summer to pick berries and dig clams.

The new Browns Point light could be seen in thin fog, but thick fog was a problem. In 1895 the Lighthouse Board reported, "In addition to the stake light [post light] at this important turning point of the numerous watercrafts plying between Tacoma and points down the sound, a fog signal is urgently needed."

Though the board saw it as an urgent need, Congress did not. It took five years for $6,000 to be appropriated for purchase of the land and construction of the station. When it was completed, a small dwelling for one keeper and his family stood a short distance from a two-story wooden tower. A fog bell was suspended in a cutout beneath the tower's roof, with a lens lantern below the bell.

On October 26, 1903, just hours before the light was scheduled to be lit, keeper Oscar V. Brown and his wife, Annie, arrived on the tender *Heather* from the Smith Island Lighthouse. Born in New York, Brown had worked for the Lighthouse Service since 1890, and had also served at Cape Flattery and New Dungeness. At dusk he lit the Browns Point light and wrote in the log, "The lamp and fog bell in good working order."

According to Mavis Stears in her book, *Two Points of View*, the tender carried the Browns' furniture, a horse and cow, and a piano.

The horse and cow were unloaded in a sling and swam to land. Once the piano was ashore, the ship's crew left. The piano, too heavy for Brown to move into the dwelling, stood outside until help came from Tacoma.

When the Browns arrived they had no neighbors, but people soon began building summer cottages on the beach near the lighthouse, followed by permanent homes on the hill above. Brown, a large, gentle man who wore a bushy mustache, was a favorite with local children. He wore his uniform when the lighthouse tender arrived, and when he gave tours. At other times he wore bib overalls. An accomplished pianist, he gave lessons when he wasn't tending the light.

The tower stood at the edge of the beach, where Brown had to row to it at high tide until the grounds were graded and filled in 1906. A half hour before sunset, he would climb the stairs inside the tower to the attic where the lens lantern rested on a sliding shelf. He would light the lamp, then push the shelf outside.

In a 1913 newspaper article, Brown said that on foggy nights when the bell rang, he usually lay awake in bed because the fog bell clockworks "must be wound up at regular intervals of three-quarters of an hour. So when the bell rings at night, I have to climb up here [in the tower] often enough to wind the mechanism." When the clockworks failed, the Browns kept the bell clanging. Annie timed the strikes — one every two seconds — and Oscar hit the bell with a sledgehammer.

In the same article, Oscar Brown said that lighthouse visitors often remarked, "What a grand summer home." But Brown told the reporter that his life was "not the summer vacation some persons think it is." At the one-keeper station, Brown was on duty twenty-four hours a day and did not have a vacation for ten years.

Life became a little easier for Brown in 1922, when electricity was installed at the station. A blinking floodlight replaced the lens lantern, and the fog bell clockworks were wound by an electric motor. Brown could operate both with switches in the dwelling.

TED NELSON

At Browns Point, temporary "lighthouse keepers" can spend a week living in the turn-of-the-century keeper's dwelling.

Occasionally Brown's routine of hard-working days and nights was spiced with culture. Both he and Annie enjoyed music. They often took the last boat to Tacoma for a concert in town, and returned home by walking across the tide flats and over the hill to the point.

In 1933, while Brown was still keeper, the wooden tower was burned down to make way for the present thirty-one-foot concrete tower. The old fog bell, which was replaced by an electrically operated foghorn, now hangs in a church on Fox Island.

Brown retired after serving forty-nine years with the Lighthouse Service. He and Annie moved to Tacoma.

Cyril Beaulieu became the chief lighthouse keeper in 1944, and two coast guardsmen assisted him. Beaulieu started with the

Lighthouse Service in 1930 and had served at the Destruction Island, Patos Island, Slip Point, and Mukilteo lighthouses. After he retired in 1956, three coast guardsmen manned the station and tended minor lights around Tacoma's Commencement Bay. They left when the station was automated in 1963.

The station is now leased by the Coast Guard to Tacoma's Metropolitan Parks District. The Points Northeast Historical Society is custodian for the dwelling, the boathouse, and the old Coast Guard crew quarters, which houses a history center and museum.

In the fall of 1998, the society opened the dwelling under a program called "Lighthouse Keepers Tour of Duty." The dwelling's upstairs and kitchen are furnished for guests who stay a week for a fee. The downstairs, furnished in the style of the 1900s, is a museum.

Directions and Hours

From Exit 137 off I-5, go north on 54th Avenue NE to SR 509 (Marine View Drive). Follow SR 509 about 5.3 miles to the junction with Le-Lou-Wa Place at a small shopping center. Then follow the yellow line on Le-Lou-Wa Place to the lighthouse parking area.

The park is open year-round, dawn to dusk. Buildings are open Sat. 1-4, closed Thanksgiving to Feb. 1.

For information about being a "keeper," call (253) 927-2536.

7. Dofflemyer Point Lighthouse

Near Tacoma, the waters of Puget Sound ebb and flow through a passage called the Tacoma Narrows. To the south, the sound spreads around islands and into inlets and small bays. In the late 1880s the Lighthouse Service began hanging lens lanterns on posts to mark prominent points and passages in the south sound.

The Lighthouse Board described these post lights as "of much use during fog, as the lights can be seen, except in very dense fog, at a distance of 100 yards or more." Without their aid, boats could not run at night.

Dofflemyer Point Lighthouse, near Olympia, began as one of these post lights in 1887. Today the point's small concrete tower with a light and fog signal, built in 1933-1934, is on the National Register of Historic Places. It is not considered a lighthouse in the strictest sense, because this aid to navigation was tended only by contract keepers for a hundred years.

Named for a pioneer homesteader, Dofflemyer Point is on the northeast corner of Budd Inlet. The post light there was first established on a wharf. Fuel for the lamp was periodically delivered by lighthouse tender.

The first known contract keeper was Leonard Sperring. When he retired in 1912, Edward R. Robinson, whose home was on the point, took his place. While Robinson was keeper, the present thirty-four-foot-high tower was constructed. It held an electric light and an air horn fog signal.

Over the years, care of the light became a neighborhood affair. When Edward Robinson retired in 1942 his son Robert, who lived next door, became the contract keeper. During the 1960s, the Coast

TED NELSON

This small concrete tower, built at Dofflemyer Point in the 1930s, is on the National Register of Historic Places.

Guard automated the light but not the fog signal, and in 1965 Madeline Campbell became the keeper. She, her husband, and their children lived in the house once owned by Edward Robinson.

While the light turned on and off automatically, a contract keeper was still required to activate the fog signal and to do minor repairs on the facility. Registered as the official "lamplighter," Mrs. Campbell sent monthly reports to the Coast Guard about lighthouse activity and the times that the fog signal was on. The Campbells activated the signal when fog crept around the point and visibility dropped. They turned it off when they could see the shoreline across the inlet.

If the Campbells expected fog to form after they went to bed, Mrs. Campbell would set the alarm clock so they could check weather conditions in the middle of the night. Taking responsibility for the fog horn was like having a young child. When the family left home, "we had to get a fog horn 'sitter,'" Mrs. Campbell said, "and the neighbors were always good about doing it."

If repairs were needed, her husband and son helped. When the light bulb went out, they would change it. This task usually occurred, she said, "in the worst time of the year."

After twenty years of service, Mrs. Campbell received a pin of recognition from the Coast Guard. Even after the fog signal was automated, she kept an eye on the tower from her front room window. If anything was amiss, she informed the Coast Guard.

But now Mrs. Campbell no longer worries about the light. She said, "The light and fog signal are working efficiently, and they don't seem to need that much attention."

Directions and Hours

The tower and grounds are not accessible to the public, but the tower can be seen from near Boston Harbor to the north.

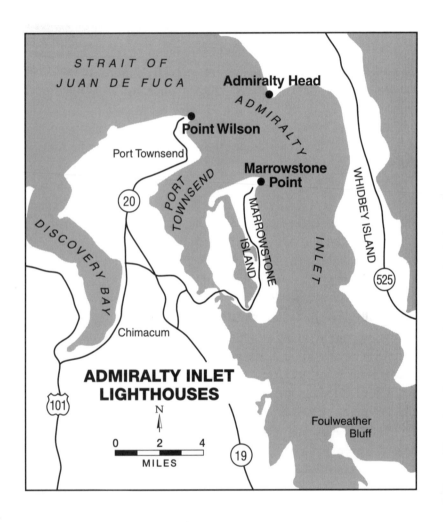

STRAIT OF
JUAN DE FUCA

Admiralty Head

ADMIRALTY

Point Wilson

Port Townsend

PORT TOWNSEND

Marrowstone
Point

MARROWSTONE ISLAND

WHIDBEY ISLAND

20

DISCOVERY BAY

INLET

525

Chimacum

**ADMIRALTY INLET
LIGHTHOUSES**

N

101

0   2   4

MILES

19

Foulweather
Bluff

GUARDIANS OF ADMIRALTY INLET

Admiralty Inlet extends south from the Strait of Juan de Fuca to the head of Puget Sound near Foulweather Bluff. The inlet, named by Captain George Vancouver in 1792, is about fourteen miles long and three to six miles wide. It is bounded on the east by Whidbey Island and on the west by the bay at Port Townsend, Marrowstone Island, and the entrance to Hood Canal.

By the 1860s, the Lighthouse Board had built five lighthouses along the Washington coast and the Strait of Juan de Fuca. With more ships sailing to Puget Sound, lighthouses were needed along Admiralty Inlet.

Three light stations were established, the first on Admiralty Head on Whidbey Island. Though decommissioned after sixty-one years of operation, a lighthouse built there still stands. The other two, Point Wilson Lighthouse near Port Townsend and Marrowstone Point Lighthouse on Marrowstone Island, are still operating.

In the late 1890s, the Coast Artillery Corps built three forts to provide a "triangle of fire" over Admiralty Inlet to defend Puget Sound. This fit the triangular pattern that the Lighthouse Board used to guide mariners through the inlet. Fort Casey was built at Admiralty Head; Fort Worden was built near Point Wilson Lighthouse; and Fort Flagler was built near Marrowstone Point Lighthouse. Today abandoned gun emplacements can be seen near these lighthouses.

FIRST LIGHTHOUSE, at

ADMIRALTY HEAD

Built in 1861, the first lighthouse on Admiralty Head was a popular social spot, attracting many Sunday visitors.

8. Admiralty Head Lighthouse

Two lighthouses stood on Admiralty Head. The first, built in 1861, is gone. The second was decommissioned in 1922 and is now an interpretive center in Fort Casey State Park on Whidbey Island.

In the mid-1800s most ships plying Washington's waters were sailing vessels. Those inbound on the Strait of Juan de Fuca passed the New Dungeness light. Then captains steered a course for Admiralty Head to clear Point Wilson and its shallow waters. Near Admiralty Head, vessels turned south into Admiralty Inlet.

The Lighthouse Board reported in 1860 that "the lighthouse at Whidby's [sic] island, provided for by the act of August 18, 1856, is in course of erection. . . ." When completed, the white, two-story wooden dwelling surrounded by a picket fence was perched near the edge of a ninety-foot-high bluff. Rising from the dwelling was a tower with a red-roofed lantern. On January 21, 1861, a fixed-white light was displayed from a fourth-order Fresnel lens. The *Coast Pilot* described the light: "It illuminates an arc of 270 degrees of the horizon and commands Admiralty Inlet and the approaches."

The first keeper was William Robertson. A "gray, grizzled sea dog," as one writer affectionately called him, Robertson had owned and sailed a vessel carrying piling from Neah Bay to San Francisco. He, his wife, and five children moved from a log cabin on the island to the lighthouse. While Robertson served as keeper, he also served as the county coroner.

Robertson was replaced by Daniel Pearson in 1865. Pearson had come west for his health, bringing his two eldest daughters, Josephine and Georgia. Shortly after they arrived, Josephine died. Following the tragedy, Daniel moved from Port Gamble to join

Georgia, a schoolteacher on Whidbey Island. Daniel then became principal keeper, and his daughter Georgia his assistant keeper.

About a year later, Pearson's wife and their two youngest children, Daniel and Flora, arrived from Massachusetts. In her memoirs Flora described the homey sight that greeted them. Chickens scratched about in the yard while pigs and cows lolled about in pens. Inside, the table was set with a meal prepared from fresh eggs, milk, and golden butter.

With two marriageable daughters at the lighthouse, many bachelors visited to attend a party or to listen to Flora play the piano. One Sunday, according to Flora, "There were fifteen horses with men's saddles on their backs, hitched to the fence." In 1866 Georgia's wedding was held in the lighthouse parlor.

Seventeen-year-old Flora succeeded Georgia as the assistant keeper. For their work Flora received $625 annually, and her father was paid $1,000. Flora kept the lighthouse log, and her entry for January 2, 1876, read: "During the last week the wind has blown continuously—first from the south—then from the west—blowing a perfect gale all the time. Flag staff blown down. On Thursday night last the bark *Windward* loaded with lumber from Seattle, bound for San Francisco, ran ashore in Useless Bay, mistaking a fire on the beach in that vicinity for Admiralty Head Light."

Her entry on May 8, 1876, was not about ships or winds, but about marriage. "Assistant Keeper lighthouse [Flora] arrived at Victoria in the p.m. and was married by Rev. W. Ross in the evening." Flora's groom was William B. Engle, a Whidbey Island pioneer. They honeymooned in San Francisco, then returned to the lighthouse where Flora resumed her duties. In September 1877 the Engles' first child was born at the lighthouse.

The elder Pearson bought a farm on Whidbey Island and resigned from lightkeeping in October 1878. Flora resigned a month later, and she and her husband and child joined her parents on the farm.

After the Pearsons, two more lightkeepers served in the wooden

Admiralty Head's second lighthouse before it was decommissioned in 1922. Today it is an interpretive center.

lighthouse. Laurence Nessel, a bachelor, served for ten years. His entries, usually brief compared with Flora's, described lighthouse chores and the weather. On April 13, 1880, Nessel noted the arrival of the Lighthouse Service tender *Shubrick* with a lampist on board who "changed the oil lamp for a kerosene lamp."

Nessel was replaced by J. E. Evans, a former cavalry officer. While Evans was keeper, the government bought lands adjoining the lighthouse and began building Fort Casey. Because the lighthouse stood on the site designated for a gun emplacement, it was moved away from the bluff and served as a medical clinic and noncommissioned officers' quarters. Later, the old lighthouse was dismantled and its timbers used to build a home on Useless Bay.

Admiralty Head's second lighthouse was built by the War Department. When Fort Casey was completed, its batteries lined

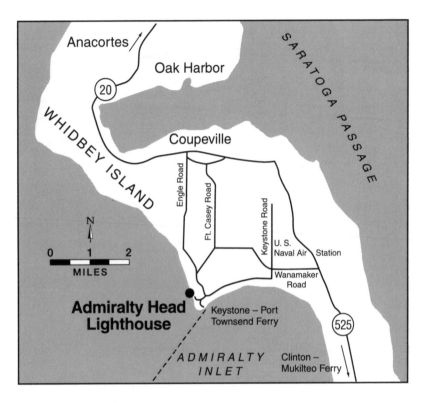

the bluff. The second lighthouse stood north of the bluff, on the slope above the fort. Its design, unique among West Coast lighthouses, set the tower at one corner of a spacious two-story brick and stucco dwelling. The Lighthouse Board reported that on June 24, 1903, "The light was . . . moved and established without change in the characteristic, in new station."

Yet the change from sailing ships to steamships soon made the new lighthouse unnecessary; steamships sailing a more north-south route near the inlet's western shore could be guided by the Point Wilson light. Admiralty Head's light was extinguished in 1922.

The lens and lantern were removed five years later, and the lantern was installed on the newly shortened tower of New Dungeness. Then the lighthouse stood vacant until World War II.

At the onset of the war, Fort Casey was reactivated as a training center, and a K-9 (dog patrol) sentry unit was stationed at the fort. For an unpublished master's thesis about Fort Casey, Terry Buchanan interviewed Private Donald Sutton, who was assigned to the K-9 unit in 1943. Sutton stated, "Because our work was all at night everyone in the detail was moved out of the regular barracks and into the empty lighthouse." There Sutton and the others could sleep peacefully during the day.

After the war, the lighthouse, painted a drab camouflage green and its lantern and lens gone, stood empty again. In the 1950s the lighthouse and the fort became a Washington state park.

Park personnel moved into the lighthouse temporarily and helped Island County residents restore it. A new lantern was installed on the tower, and the lighthouse was opened as an interpretive center, with the Fresnel lens used at the Alki Point Lighthouse on display.

When Washington lighthouses were dismantled or became victims of erosion, usually they were replaced by newer aids to navigation. However, the light at Admiralty Head, like the sailing vessels it served, never shone again.

The Admiralty Head Lighthouse had been deleted from official light lists for nearly seventy years when it received national recognition in 1990. It and four other lighthouses were featured on a United States Postal Service stamp issue commemorating the United States Coast Guard's bicentennial. Admiralty Head was the only West Coast lighthouse featured.

Directions and Hours

Access to the lighthouse is through Fort Casey State Park; phone (360) 678-4519. The lighthouse is open April-May, Thur.-Sun., 11-5; June-Sept., Wed.-Sun. 11-5; Thanksgiving weekend, Fri.-Sun., 11-4; Dec., Sat.-Sun. 11-4 until Christmas. Phone (360) 679-7391. At other times the lighthouse can be viewed from the outside.

A Fresnel lens in the tower of Point Wilson's second lighthouse still guides mariners in Admiralty Inlet and the Strait of Juan de Fuca.

9. Point Wilson Lighthouse

Point Wilson is a broad, sandy point about two miles northwest of Port Townsend. Vessels plying the Strait of Juan de Fuca and Admiralty Inlet turn at this point, where a light has been guiding mariners since 1879. As one coast guardsman said with a touch of nostalgia, "This is one lighthouse where you can still see the classical Fresnel lens."

Early surveys cited two locations for lighthouses at the entrance to Admiralty Inlet, one on the west shore at Point Wilson and one on the east shore on Whidbey Island. At the time, Port Townsend was the port of entry for Washington Territory, and the town's citizens wanted a lighthouse. However, the Lighthouse Board chose Whidbey Island's Admiralty Head instead.

The absence of a light or fog signal at Point Wilson prompted one mariner to act. In 1865, shortly after St. Paul's Episcopal Church was built in Port Townsend, Captain J. W. Seldon donated a ship's bell to the church. The gift came on one condition — the bell had to be rung on foggy days.

Several years later, the clanging bell guided a steamer into Port Townsend, saving it from going aground. An evangelist on board was so grateful that he wrote a hymn, "The Harbor Bell," which appeared in songbooks for many years.

Two hundred seventy-two vessels entered Port Townsend in 1871, and traffic continued to increase. It wasn't until 1879, however, that sufficient funds were appropriated to establish a lighthouse and fog signal on the point. On December 15 of that year, keeper Laurence Nessel at Admiralty Head looked across the inlet and wrote in his log, "Light at Point Wilson in operation for first time."

A fourth-order Fresnel lens showing a fixed-white light was mounted in a square tower that projected from the keepers' one-and-one-half-story wooden dwelling. Its light could be seen to a distance of thirteen miles. A nearby fog signal building housed boilers and a twelve-inch steam whistle. The first two keepers were David Littlefield and his assistant H. L. Rogers, who had transferred from the Smith Island Lighthouse.

Littlefield, a Civil War veteran, had arrived in Port Townsend in 1867 and married Maria Hastings, the eldest daughter of a Port Townsend pioneer. After four years at Point Wilson, the Littlefields settled in Port Townsend, where David later served as sheriff of Jefferson County and mayor of Port Townsend. In 1887 the couple built a home overlooking the town's harbor. It still stands and is a private residence.

When Littlefield left the lighthouse, his then assistant, W. H. Jankins, was promoted to principal keeper. Six months later Jankins moved to the Point No Point Lighthouse, and George Draper took over as principal keeper at Point Wilson.

In 1894 the Lighthouse Service repaired the old fog signal boiler, and, the board reported, "A new lens with revolving apparatus was substituted for the old one." This revolving lens with a red screen projected a fixed-white light interrupted by short flashes of red.

Two years later, construction of Fort Worden began on the bluffs west of the lighthouse. Gun emplacements and a lookout tower were built among the sand dunes. From the tower, which is still standing, sentries could scan surrounding waters for 270 degrees.

In 1914 the present lighthouse was built, closer to the end of the point. The tower, rising from a fog-signal building, was designed in an octagonal shape to reduce wind pressure. The Fresnel lens was placed in the tower's lantern, forty-six feet above the ground. The old tower was removed from atop the remodeled dwelling, which continued to serve as a home for the keepers.

During World War I, lighthouse keepers were encouraged to

COAST GUARD MUSEUM NORTHWEST

The revenue cutter *Snohomish* steams by the first lighthouse on Point Wilson, circa 1890.

grow their own food to support the war effort. In 1917 keeper William J. Thomas wrote to the lighthouse inspector in Portland, Oregon, "I have sent you today per parcel post a sample of some of the vegetables I raised at the station here." The package included peas, potatoes, and carrots. Thomas continued, "Early onions and lettuce were splendid: gave [lighthouse tender] *Heather* some for their mess."

One of Thomas's most crucial moments would come four years later. On the foggy morning of April 1, 1921, Thomas was on watch when he heard ships collide and immediately called Port Townsend for assistance. The steamers *Governor* and *Hartland* had crashed, and the *Governor* sank. Nine lives were lost, but more people might have died if not for Thomas's quick response.

After 1939 Coast Guard keepers tended the light and fog signal until automation came in 1976. Later a tower-mounted radar unit was built at the station. It tracks vessel movement and sends the information to the Puget Sound Vessel Traffic Service in Seattle.

The dwelling, once occupied by David Littlefield and his family, now serves as apartments for the families of two coast guardsmen assigned to the cutter *Point Bennett* out of Port Townsend. Fort Worden is a Washington state park; its grounds, gun emplacements, and quarters were the setting for the movie *An Officer and a Gentleman.* Restored barracks and officers' quarters, used for guest housing during conferences, are also available to rent.

Directions and Hours

In the summer of 1998, the Coast Guard was concluding negotiations with the Washington State Parks and Recreation Commission to make the 1914 lighthouse a part of Fort Worden State Park. The lighthouse will then be open to the public under the auspices of the Jefferson County Historical Society. For current information call the Jefferson County Historical Museum at (360) 385-1003.

When not open, the lighthouse can be seen by taking an easy walk around the point.

Access is through Fort Worden State Park. Phone: (360) 385-4730. In Port Townsend, follow signs to Fort Worden State Park. Proceed past the fort's parade grounds to parking near the beach and point. Park hours are: April 1 - October 15, 6:30-dusk. Rest of year, 8-dusk.

10. Marrowstone Point Lighthouse

Marrowstone Point, at the northeast end of Marrowstone Island, was named by Captain George Vancouver after the soft clay he saw on the bluff.

Its station began as a post light in 1888. A lens lantern showing red hung from a white post on the beach and was tended by a contract keeper. In 1896 the Lighthouse Service added a fog bell, and a resident keeper and his family moved into a one-and-one-half-story, wood-frame dwelling.

Though living on an island, the keeper and his family had little chance to be lonely. Within a year after they moved to the point, construction of Fort Flagler began on the bluffs above. By 1900 the armament was in place and men of the 3rd Artillery moved into temporary barracks. The fort was completed in 1907.

Beaches near the lighthouse station became popular with both soldiers from the fort and with island residents who came to fish for salmon. For years Marrowstone Point Fishing Resort stood near the lighthouse.

In 1907 Axel Rustad was transferred from Ediz Hook Lighthouse to Marrowstone Point. He and his family became friends with island residents, who often came calling after church on summer Sundays in horse-drawn carriages.

Like fog bells at other lighthouses, Marrowstone's brought complaints from mariners. In 1913 an experimental fog signal, a gun fired at intervals, was installed — but the experiment was unsuccessful. Five years later a small fog signal building was constructed to house compressors for a Daboll trumpet, and an electric light was placed on the top.

The beaches around the Marrowstone Point Lighthouse were popular with soldiers stationed at Fort Flagler on the bluff above.

In the 1920s Rustad was replaced by Jacob Hall, who brought his wife and three sons to live at the lighthouse until 1938. Hall then transferred to West Point, where he served for a year before retiring after twenty-six years with the Lighthouse Service.

Coast guardsmen lived at the station until the light and a modern fog signal were automated in 1962. Today some of the original buildings still stand on the site. The United States Fish and Wildlife Service now uses the keeper's dwelling as a laboratory. Lab equipment fills rooms where the keeper, his wife, and his children once lived.

A military post until 1955, Fort Flagler is now a Washington State Park. Visitors can stay in the barracks or walk the beach near the lighthouse station grounds, which are closed to the public.

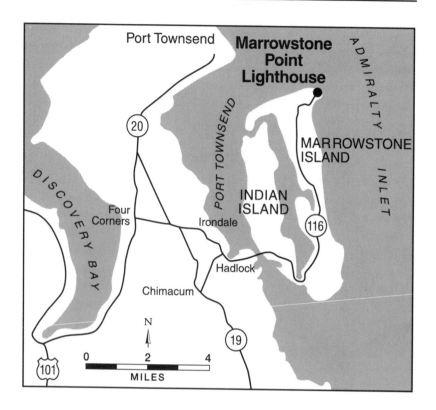

Directions and Hours

Access to the lighthouse is through Fort Flagler State Park. The park is open April 15 to Oct. 1, from 6-dusk. Rest of year, 8-dusk. Phone: (360) 385-1259.

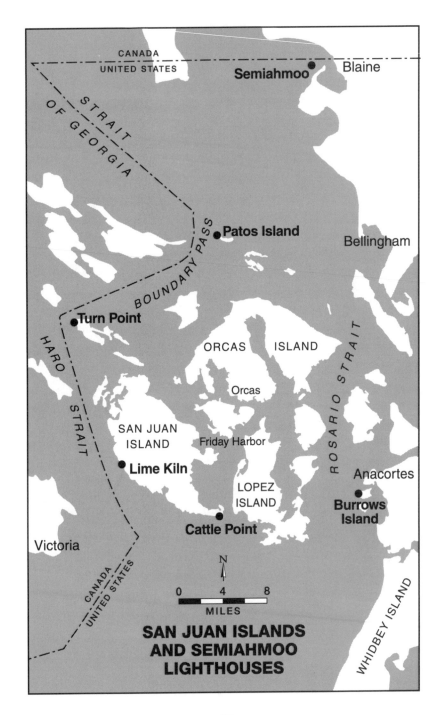

CANADA
UNITED STATES

STRAIT OF GEORGIA

Semiahmoo

Blaine

Patos Island

Bellingham

BOUNDARY PASS

Turn Point

HARO STRAIT

ORCAS ISLAND

Orcas

SAN JUAN ISLAND

Friday Harbor

Lime Kiln

LOPEZ ISLAND

ROSARIO STRAIT

Anacortes

Burrows Island

Victoria

CANADA
UNITED STATES

Cattle Point

N

0   4   8
MILES

WHIDBEY ISLAND

**SAN JUAN ISLANDS
AND SEMIAHMOO
LIGHTHOUSES**

SAN JUAN SENTINELS

The San Juans, an archipelago of more than 170 islands, were explored in the 1790s by Manuel Quimper, a Spanish seafarer. Years later, the islands' passages and coves were used by smugglers dealing in Chinese laborers, diamonds, and liquor.

For a time both Americans and British occupied the islands, which led to the 1859 armed dispute known as the "Pig War." After the controversy was resolved in 1872, the United States took possession of the islands.

Then the Secretary of the Interior asked the Lighthouse Board if there were any tracts in the islands "which it desired to have reserved for lighthouse purposes?" Unfamiliar with the islands and working from charts, the board selected twenty-three sites, "to provide for all probable events." Lime Kiln, Cattle Point, Patos Island, and Turn Point were among the locations chosen.

Four lighthouses at these sites and one at Burrows Island still guide mariners through the straits and passages around the islands. The importance of these island lighthouses was emphasized by the *Coast Pilot*, which stated that "Owing to the variable direction and velocity of the currents, compass courses are of little value." Today commercial vessels sail past the lighthouses, and pleasure boaters find moorage in the coves once frequented by smugglers.

North of the San Juans, Semiahmoo Lighthouse (now gone) marked shallows near Blaine, Washington.

11. Cattle Point Lighthouse

The Cattle Point Lighthouse is on San Juan Island, for which the archipelago is named. In the 1850s, Britain's Hudson's Bay Company grazed sheep and cattle near Cattle Point at the island's southern end. A few Americans settled nearby.

The joint occupancy took place while the two countries were trying to peacefully determine which of them would own the archipelago. The dispute arose because of vague language in the 1846 treaty that established the boundary between Canada and the United States.

In 1859 an American killed a pig belonging to the Hudson's Bay Company. An international crisis developed, with troops from the two countries manning an "American Camp" and an "English Camp." British warships patrolled the waters. In 1872, Germany's Kaiser Wilhelm I arbitrated the dispute, ruling in favor of the United States.

Cattle Point's first light was a lens lantern on a post erected in 1888. The first known contract keeper was George Jakle.

Jakle's father had been a soldier at American Camp. When his enlistment was up, he remained on the island and farmed near the present lighthouse. During the early 1900s, George Jakle lived on the family farm and raised sheep on the grasslands while serving as keeper.

In 1989, eighty-three-year-old Kenneth Dougherty, who grew up near the point, recalled watching Jakle carry out his lightkeeping duties. Every few months, a lighthouse tender steamed into Griffin Bay on the island's southeast side and unloaded several five-gallon barrels of kerosene on the beach. "Jakle went down with his horse and buggy, loaded up the barrels, and hauled them home," said

On a bluff on San Juan Island, the Cattle Point Lighthouse is a welcome sight for boaters after crossing the Strait of Juan de Fuca.

Dougherty. "He had to fill the lantern once a week and carried the barrels on horseback. A lot of times [the light] went out, and he'd go down and light it again."

In 1921, the United States Navy installed a radio compass station near the light. Using radio signals from Cattle Point, Smith Island, and New Dungeness, mariners sailing in the thickest fog along the Strait of Juan de Fuca could determine their locations.

Ethel Martin visited the station often while she was being courted by a young Navy cook, Kenneth Martin, Sr., assigned there in 1924. They enjoyed picnic lunches prepared by Kenneth, whom Ethel eventually married.

She remembered a barracks where four sailors lived, and a separate house for the chief and his wife. "The Navy was taking care of the light," she said. The sailors walked a wooden pathway from the station to the light.

During the 1930s, the radio compass station was closed. Some of the buildings burned down, and others were razed. All that remains is the shell of the concrete power plant building and the

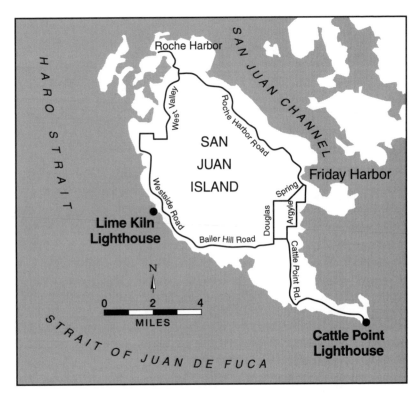

foundation for the radio tower. The concrete shell serves as a sheltered picnic area on the Cattle Point Interpretive Trail. From there trails lead down to the beach and through the dunes where Jakle's sheep once grazed, and to the bluff where the lighthouse stands.

The lens lantern on a post was replaced in 1935 by the present thirty-four-foot-high concrete tower. Today solar-powered batteries operate a small modern optic and a fog signal. Standing prominently on a bluff, the Cattle Point Lighthouse is a welcome sight for pleasure boaters arriving at the San Juans after crossing the Strait of Juan de Fuca.

Directions and Hours:

The small tower can be reached by taking a short hike from a parking area near the end of Cattle Point Road.

12. Lime Kiln Lighthouse

The Lime Kiln Lighthouse is on the west side of San Juan Island, overlooking the entrance to Haro Strait. When the Lighthouse Board considered this site for a lighthouse in 1875, the point was nameless and identified only as "south of Ship Trees" — trees that provided a reference point for early mariners entering the strait. The point was later named for the lime kilns built nearby in the 1860s. The remains of an early lime kiln and quarry are just north of the light.

A light has shown from this low, rocky bluff since 1914. The present lighthouse — a small, concrete fog signal building with a tower — began operation June 30, 1919. A fourth-order Fresnel lens displayed a flashing white light. This was the last major light established in Washington, and the two original keepers' dwellings still stand on the hillside above the lighthouse.

An incandescent oil vapor lamp served as the light source until the mid-1940s, when electricity finally came to the lighthouse. Power to the station had been delayed, because the local power company could not provide sufficient current, and installation costs were prohibitive since the poles had to be set in solid rock.

Helga Settles remembered life at the station without electricity. She, her lightkeeper husband, Arvel, and their five children moved to Lime Kiln in 1935. In a 1989 interview, she said, "I washed on a scrub board, and we wound the mechanism to turn the light by hand."

Arvel, a World War I veteran, joined the Lighthouse Service in 1920. He and Helga moved into their first lighthouse at Point Arguello, California, where their home was rent free, and he was paid $87 a month. Three assignments later, the Settles arrived at

CARL MONTFORD

Washington's last major light was established at Lime Kiln Point in 1914. It is now a center for the study of killer whales.

Washington's Grays Harbor Lighthouse in 1926. There their son Jack developed asthma. The district lighthouse superintendent suggested the family move to Lime Kiln for its drier climate. They did, and Jack recovered — "So well that he joined the Navy," said Helga.

Despite the lack of electricity, Helga "enjoyed every bit of living at Lime Kiln." She had a vegetable garden and was an expert at growing flowers. The most difficult thing was keeping house. "We had to keep our houses really clean for the inspector," explained Helga. This meant a clean house every day, since they never knew when the lighthouse inspector would come.

The children rode the school bus to attend school in Friday Harbor. Though Helga didn't help her husband with lighthouse duties, the children often did, because their father would give them ten cents to wind the clockwork mechanism that rotated the lens.

Charles, the Settleses' youngest son, recalled his days at Lime Kiln as a teenager. "We were out on the water a lot," said Charles.

"When old boats washed up on shore, Jack and I would rejuvenate them. We plugged the holes in the boats with rags, then covered the rags with boiled pitch. We used an oar for a rudder and made sails from gunnysacks."

Jack and Charles caught fish for the cookhouse at the lime kiln and quarry camp, and traded fish for fresh pies. One day the boys were out rowing when a small whale pursued them. They saw his fin come close, and, "Oh, did we go! We made the water fly," said Charles. The whale got caught in kelp, and the boys scrambled ashore.

The Settleses left the lighthouse in 1942 and moved to Friday Harbor. A modern optic and the fog signal were automated in 1962.

Although only one whale chased Charles and Jack, many whales, including orca and minke whales, swim in the waters off the point. Whale Watch Park was dedicated in 1985 as a place to watch and study them. The lighthouse became a research station for marine mammal scientists.

Directions and Hours:

The Lime Kiln Lighthouse can be viewed from the outside. Access to it and Whale Watch Park is through Lime Kiln State Park, open from sunrise to sunset. For current information, call the state park at (360) 378-2044. (See map on page 64.)

13. Turn Point Lighthouse

On the northwest end of Stuart Island, Turn Point (as the name implies) is a point where ships change course when sailing Haro Strait and Boundary Pass.

Recognizing this, the Lighthouse Board established a lighthouse station there, which began operation on November 30, 1893. A lens lantern was mounted on a small building housing a Daboll trumpet fog signal. A large, two-story keepers' dwelling was built uphill from the point.

Three years later, Edward Durgan became principal keeper, and Peter Christiansen his assistant. On a stormy February night in 1897, the two heard distress signals. The steamer *Enterprise* had foundered on the point. Risking their own lives in the frigid waters, Durgan and Christiansen rescued all on board.

The keepers received a certificate of merit which read, "Such services to humanity merit the highest commendation and the [Lighthouse] Board is glad to number among its employees men of such sterling courage and fidelity. . . ."

In 1918 keeper L. A. Borchers received a commendation of another kind. During World War I, there was a national effort to conserve food, so Borchers in one season canned 311 cans of fish including sockeye and pink salmon, sardines, and salmon caviar. The Bureau of Fisheries examined samples and found them "to be of high quality . . . and compared favorably with commercial products."

Borchers's achievement did not go unnoticed. Herbert Hoover, then United States Food Administrator, wrote a letter to the Secretary of Commerce stating that Borchers had shown "what can be

Two lightkeepers at Turn Point risked their lives to rescue all on board the vessel *Enterprise* on a stormy night in 1897.

accomplished 'where raw material swims past the door' . . . in view of the amount of work which I know is necessary for a lightkeeper to perform in the course of his regular duties."

When the Lighthouse Service was absorbed by the Coast Guard, the young recruits assigned to Turn Point had neither the skill nor the interest of the early Lighthouse Service keepers. Most were bored with lighthouse duty and anxiously awaited shore leave in Bellingham.

After World War II, the Coast Guard classified Turn Point as a "family station." Coast guardsman Dan Alexander learned this when he applied for duty there in 1949. Alexander, engaged to be married several months later, moved up his wedding date to qualify for the position. On their honeymoon, he and his bride moved into one side of the keepers' dwelling, which they shared with a bachelor keeper. The head keeper, Edward S. Swanson, and his wife lived on the other side.

By then the light and fog signal had been upgraded: an electric light was mounted on top of a short tower, and a modern fog signal rattled the keepers' dishes when it blew.

The Alexanders' first winter at the station was one of the harshest on record. A spring-fed water system froze. Dan crawled into a 20,000-gallon tank and chopped a hole through one-foot-thick ice. For weeks, he and his wife hand-carried water to the dwelling.

The couple's groceries came from the one store in Friday Harbor. They would radio their list to a Coast Guard cutter, and the groceries were boxed up at the store and delivered by mail boat to the island's Prevost Harbor. The couple remembered "getting day-old bread and dented cans from the store, but our milk, eggs, and butter were fresh from a small farm on the island." In 1997 the Alexanders celebrated forty-eight years of marriage.

The station was automated in 1974. Today a solar-electric system provides energy to a modern optic and fog signal, which are maintained by the Aids to Navigation Team Puget Sound, Seattle. The original keepers' dwelling, subject to vandalism in past years, has been boarded up.

Directions and Hours

Access to the Turn Point Lighthouse is by boat. Anchor in Stuart Island's Prevost Harbor and hike the two-mile-long trail to the point. The lighthouse can also be reached from Reid Harbor, but the trail is longer, and the first mile is poorly marked.

14. Patos Island Lighthouse

Spanish explorers named this small island on the northern edge of the San Juans *Isla de Patos*, or "Island of Ducks." It faces Boundary Pass, a busy waterway connecting Haro Strait with Canada's Strait of Georgia.

In the 1880s steamships bound for Alaska and Canada and coal ships sailing from Nanaimo, British Columbia, often encountered fog along this waterway. Many of these were American ships, and in 1890 the Lighthouse Board recommended "a post light and first class Daboll trumpet in duplicate" be established on the west end of the island. On November 30, 1893, a light and fog signal began operation at Patos Island and also at Turn Point on Stuart Island, along the same waterway.

Life at the Patos Island Lighthouse in the early 1900s was described by Helene Glidden in her book, *Light on the Island.* Helene moved there in 1905 with her mother, twelve brothers and sisters, and her father, lightkeeper Edward Durgan. Prior to this station, he had served at Oregon's Coquille River and Heceta Head lighthouses, and Washington's Turn Point and New Dungeness lighthouses.

Although their new home was isolated, the children found much to do. They roamed the 210-acre island, exploring caves and tide pools. The older children fished from the station's boat. And they helped tend the chickens, cows, ducks, and pigs which provided the family with fresh eggs, milk, and meat.

The lighthouse tender arrived occasionally, bringing fuel for the lamp and fog signal and paint for the buildings, but no groceries. So once a month, a few of the Durgans rowed and sailed the twenty-six miles to Bellingham to buy staples.

The keepers' dwelling (circa 1940—now gone) at the Patos Island Lighthouse Station overlooked a cove once used by smugglers.

When seven of the Durgan children contracted smallpox, the family's isolation proved tragic. With no way to call for medical help, Durgan flew the flag upside down to signal passing ships that the family was in distress. But help didn't come soon enough, and three of the children died.

In 1908 a Lighthouse Service crew moved in with the Durgans. While there, the crew built a new fog signal building with a thirty-eight-foot tower housing a rotating fourth-order Fresnel lens.

The coves and caves where the children played also attracted smugglers, who traveled at night using the lighthouse to guide them. When Mr. Durgan heard their boat engines at night, he hurried to the lighthouse and shouted at the smugglers, sending them back to sea. After eight years at Patos Island, when most of the children were grown, the Durgans moved to Semiahmoo Lighthouse near Blaine, Washington.

In the 1940s four single coast guardsmen were assigned to Patos Island. Unlike in earlier times, a Coast Guard cutter delivered supplies, groceries, and mail to them once a week. Later, the cutter arrived twice a week when families joined the men assigned to the station.

The children, all under school age, always had their fathers nearby. The wives liked the quiet routine so well that they often elected to remain on the island rather than take the seventy-two-hour liberty granted every three weeks.

One winter day in 1956, the coast guardsmen rescued a young Canadian fisherman whose boat had hit a reef near the island. He had been drifting helplessly on the Strait of Georgia in freezing weather for five days.

All personnel left when the station was automated in 1974. In time the vacant buildings were vandalized. The original keepers' dwelling and some outbuildings were razed in 1984. As coast guardsman Barry Knowles put it, "We bulldozed it flat." All that remains is the fog signal building with its tower and two old Coast Guard buildings. The Fresnel lens was replaced, and today a modern optic and fog signal are solar-powered.

Directions and Hours

Visitors can walk outside the lighthouse, which is in a state marine park and accessible only by boat.

15. Burrows Island Lighthouse

Burrows Island is on Rosario Strait, five miles southwest of Anacortes. The lighthouse station occupies four acres of benchland edged by low, rocky bluffs on its southwest side. It is one of the few level places on this forested island that rises steeply to a height of 650 feet. From this serene, picturesque setting, the lighthouse warns vessels of unseen hazards.

"The tides and currents here are strong and variable, and there are several dangerous reefs in the immediate vicinity," reported the Lighthouse Board in 1897, when it requested funds for a light and fog signal. Fog and smoke from forest fires often decreased visibility for the vessels, which were coming in increasing numbers, and "Burrows Island [was] a point of departure for most of the vessels plying the strait."

Fifteen thousand dollars was appropriated to build the station. On April 1, 1906, the first light was displayed from a fourth-order Fresnel lens. It showed a white light with a red sector, directed toward Allan Island and Dennis Shoal, hazards to the south.

The lighthouse is similar to the Mukilteo Lighthouse, built at the same time. Its wooden tower, attached to a fog signal building, stands thirty-four feet high to the top of the lantern. The building contained compressors to operate a Daboll trumpet. However, the trumpet was silent for the first three months, "there being no fog," according to the Lighthouse Board. The next year it blew 329 hours, and the compressors' engines consumed 215 gallons of oil.

About 1930 keeper Albert H. Johnson arrived at Burrows Island from Oregon's Heceta Head Lighthouse. He and his family, including his daughter Mary Lou, soon settled into the large two-story dwelling. Mary Lou later wrote in a newspaper article, "In the summertime when I got lonely, I would take my dogs, and we would climb the mountain which is in the middle of the island."

COAST GUARD MUSEUM NORTHWEST

The 1906 Burrows Island Lighthouse guides mariners along Rosario Strait on the east side of the San Juan Islands.

When summer ended, Mary Lou left the island to board at school in Anacortes. On Fridays Mr. Johnson picked her up in the station's boat to come home for the weekend. "Father would let me steer, and it was great fun. . . . When the weather was bad and the water rough, I would stay with a girlfriend."

Johnson later served at the Cape Flattery Lighthouse, then returned to Heceta Head in 1936. When the Coast Guard took over the Burrows Island Lighthouse, it assigned three men to the station for a two-year tour of duty. They and their families made frequent trips to shop in Anacortes. The buoy tender *Fir* stopped every eight months to deliver supplies, including fuel for the station's power-generating plant. In 1972 the lighthouse was automated and Coast Guard personnel left.

Today the lighthouse and dwelling still stand, along with a derrick that once lifted supplies from lighthouse tenders, but the station is closed to the public. The original Fresnel lens, replaced by a modern optic in the early 1990s, is at the Coast Guard Station in Port Angeles.

Now gone, the Semiahmoo Lighthouse was built on piling and operated from 1905 to 1944.

16. Semiahmoo Lighthouse

The Semiahmoo Lighthouse near Blaine, Washington, had a brief existence. Built in 1905, and also known as the Semiahmoo Harbor Lighthouse, it was discontinued after just under forty years of operation.

Blaine is near the boundary between the United Sates and Canada. South of town, shallow Drayton Harbor lies behind the long Semiahmoo Spit.

In the late 1890s a post light shone from the spit, but the Lighthouse Board deemed it "insufficient for the needs of commerce." Passenger steamers traveling between Vancouver, British Columbia, and Tacoma, Washington, called regularly at Blaine. Fishing boats docked at a large salmon cannery on the spit. These vessels had to cross shoal-filled waters, and at night or in fog it was hazardous.

Funds for a lighthouse on piling near the spit were received in 1903, and a light was first displayed from a fourth-order Fresnel lens on May 15, 1905. The lens shone from a short tower that rose from the center of an octagonal building; an attached building housed the Daboll trumpet. The station's boat was raised and lowered from davits.

In 1913, keeper Edward Durgan transferred from the Patos Island Lighthouse to Semiahmoo. After he died here in 1920, his wife, Estelle, served as keeper for a short time.

The lighthouse, discontinued by the Coast Guard in 1944, was torn down and replaced by an unmanned light and fog signal. The lens was eventually acquired by lighthouse historian James Gibbs, for display at his home on the Oregon Coast.

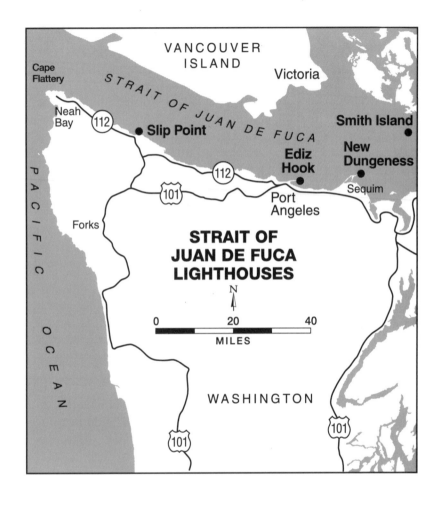

STRAIT OF
JUAN DE FUCA
LIGHTHOUSES

BEACONS OF THE STRAIT

The Strait of Juan de Fuca is named for Greek seafarer Apostolos Valerinos, also known as Juan de Fuca, who claimed to have discovered the strait in 1592 while sailing under the Spanish flag. Whether he ever saw the strait is a matter of conjecture. Nevertheless, it was named for him by British fur trader Captain Charles Barkley, who charted its entrance in 1787.

The strait connects the Pacific Ocean with the inland waters of Admiralty Inlet and Puget Sound; Washington's Olympic Mountains loom on its south shore. To the north lies Canada's Vancouver Island and passages that lead around the San Juan Islands to the Strait of Georgia. Whidbey Island bounds its eastern end. The strait is over ninety miles long and twelve to eighteen miles wide.

Winter storms intensify near the strait's entrance, causing confused seas and veering winds. In summer the strait is often blanketed by fog. The *Coast Pilot* stated that "In few parts of the world is the vigilance of the mariner more called upon than when entering the Strait of Juan de Fuca from the Pacific in the fog."

Four lighthouses were established along the strait: New Dungeness, Smith Island, Ediz Hook, and Slip Point.

"Keepers for a week," who stay in a 1905 dwelling, raise the flag at the New Dungeness Lighthouse.

17. New Dungeness Lighthouse

Since 1857, this lighthouse has marked Dungeness Spit, a low, narrow ribbon of sand curving gracefully for about five miles along the Strait of Juan de Fuca. The spit is barely visible from a distance, and several ships ran aground on the outside beach before the lighthouse was built.

The 1848 act establishing Oregon Territory (which included present-day Washington) had a provision for building lighthouses at Cape Disappointment and New Dungeness. By 1855 construction at Cape Disappointment had begun, and the Lighthouse Board was planning three more lighthouses, besides the one for New Dungeness, to be built along Washington's waters, at Willapa Bay, Cape Flattery, and Smith Island.

In its 1855-1856 annual report, the Board expressed concern that "Indian hostilities in Washington and Oregon territories and the difficulties attending operations at such distant and sparsely populated localities" could delay construction. Nevertheless, all four lighthouses were completed by 1858.

The New Dungeness Lighthouse, like the other three, was designed in the Cape Cod style, a one-and-one-half-story dwelling with a tower rising through the roof. Because this lighthouse was built on such a low spit, its tower was the highest at ninety-two feet.

The foundation and walls were built of sandstone blocks shipped from Bellingham, and the tower was made of brick with its lower half painted white and upper half painted black. Nearby, a 1,100-pound fog bell hung outside a small wooden building that housed the clockwork mechanism to operate the bell's clapper. The station began operation on December 14, 1857, displaying a fixed-white light through a third-order Fresnel lens. It was the second light-house established in what by then had become Washington Territory.

Franklin Tucker and John Tibbals served temporarily until the assigned keepers, Captain Thomas Boyling and William H. Blake, arrived at the station. Boyling, the principal keeper, served only a few months, and then Blake took Boyling's place on March 1, 1858.

Blake was a dapper twenty-one-year-old bachelor who wore a thin mustache and a small goatee. Life at the lighthouse might have been lonely had he not met the McDonnells. Richard McDonnell and his family, including his daughter Mary Ann, lived at the base of the spit. At first Blake walked to their home to help McDonnell when he was ill, then later to court Mary Ann.

In the spring of 1862, northwest pioneer and historian James Swan wrote that he "stopped for the night at the lighthouse where Mr. Blake, the keeper, treated me to supper and a share of his bed." A few months later Blake married Mary Ann, who was then eigh-teen years old.

The couple had been living at the lighthouse a short time when Mary Ann's father died. Then her mother and her four-year-old brother moved into the lighthouse, where three of the Blakes' five children were later born.

In September 1868, some Tsimshian Indian families camped near the lighthouse, on their way back to British Columbia after picking hops in the Puyallup Valley. That night Clallam Indians massacred all but one pregnant woman, who crawled to the light-house and was taken in by the Blakes. According to one account, a few days later local settlers placed the Tsimshian bodies in their canoes and set them adrift. A minor spit branching from Dungeness has since been known as Graveyard Spit.

Eventually, the Clallams involved in the attack were apprehended and placed in irons on their reservation. When the Tsimshian woman was well enough to travel, she returned home.

Years later, Richard Blake, son of William Blake, added an

intriguing postscript to the story of the massacre. An old pioneer was sitting outside a tavern in the town of Dungeness when a young Indian man rowed ashore. He asked the pioneer if he'd heard about the tragedy at the lighthouse. The pioneer said he had, and the Indian man said that he had been the baby born to the surviving Tsimshian woman.

A few weeks after the massacre, the bark *Atlanta*, outbound for San Francisco in thick fog and smoke from forest fires, went aground near the lighthouse. In a letter later written to the lighthouse inspector, the captain reported that his ship was so close to the lighthouse he could hear voices, but no fog bell was sounding. He "hailed the lighthouse keeper whom he could plainly hear talking and received no answer or assistance." As soon as the keeper saw the vessel, "He commenced ringing the bell and continued the same until he [the captain] managed by good luck to haul his vessel off." Had the bell been operating, stated the captain, his ship would have cleared the spit. The lighthouse inspector replied that he couldn't explain what had happened, but he assured the captain, "I have always found Mr. Blake a faithful and reliable keeper."

The Blakes left in late fall of 1868, and were replaced by Jacob Rogers. Other keepers served later, including Franklin Tucker, who returned in April 1873.

That same year the fog bell was retired. Like bells at other stations, it was sometimes inaudible and the striking mechanism often broke, forcing the keepers to strike the bell manually for hours. The bell was replaced by a steam whistle similar to the kind used on locomotives. Boilers for the whistle were fired by wood and coal. Later, the old fog bell was sent to the Point No Point Lighthouse.

Even with the new fog signal, shipwrecks continued to occur on Dungeness Spit. In 1894 the bark *R. K. Ham*, a veteran of one hundred trips between Puget Sound and San Francisco, commanded by Captain I. W. Gove, was inbound on a foggy August day. The ship veered slightly off course and grounded on the spit. The captain

COAST GUARD MUSEUM NORTHWEST

The New Dungeness tower was over ninety feet high before it developed cracks and the top third was removed in 1927.

and crew made it ashore and stood on the beach as the ship was pounded apart by the breakers.

By 1895 four keepers worked at New Dungeness, and the Lighthouse Service requested funds for a new dwelling. They repeated the request for several years, then finally reported, "The contractor started the work [on the dwelling] early in November 1904 and completed it in late January 1905."

This was a busy time at the lighthouse: cisterns and the original dwelling were repaired, a wharf was built into Dungeness Bay on the spit's south side, and by 1907 a new fog signal building holding oil engines and six-inch sirens was completed.

Cracks developed in the tower by 1927, and nearly thirty feet of the upper part was removed. A different-sized lantern was needed, and the one from the decommissioned Admiralty Head Lighthouse was installed. A fourth-order Fresnel lens replaced the original third-order lens.

The Fresnel lens was replaced by a modern optic in 1976, when the light and fog signal were automated. Coast Guard keeper William A. Byrd recorded his feeling of loss: "The prism lens was turned off . . . and the sparkling glass and rotating prism lens was replaced with a cold apparatus."

Once the station was automated, its staff was reduced from three to one. The keeper maintained the grounds and buildings and gave tours to visitors walking the spit.

In 1980 Seaman First Class Jeni Burr was made the lightkeeper, becoming the first woman in the Coast Guard assigned to keeper duty. She and her husband, Eric, and their five cats and two dogs moved into the 1905 dwelling. The Burrs, like the Coast Guard keepers before them, regulated their lives by the tides and weather. Since the spit is impassable to vehicles at high tide, the Burrs drove their Coast Guard jeep to and from Sequim at low tide. When storms pushed logs on shore, they had to winch them out of the way. If there were too many logs to move, they took their small boat to town and hoped the next storm would carry the logs away.

In 1994 Seth Jackson was stationed at New Dungeness with his wife, Michelle, when the Coast Guard notified him that he would be transferred. Helicopters delivered window coverings to permanently board up the station, which had become the last Coast Guard manned lighthouse on the West Coast.

Before the windows could be boarded up, however, volunteers with the Coast Guard Auxiliary made a commitment to keep the lighthouse open for the many visitors who walked along the spit. Then Sequim residents organized the New Dungeness Chapter of the United States Lighthouse Society, which leased the station from the Coast Guard.

Now people who join the chapter and pay a fee can become "keepers." On a Friday at low tide, they are driven to the station by chapter volunteers, to be picked up a week later. Like keepers before them, they stay in the 1905 dwelling, conduct tours of the tower, raise and lower the flag daily, mow the lawn, and do minor chores. The opportunity is so attractive to lighthouse enthusiasts that the reservation list is two years long.

Directions and Hours:

Access to the lighthouse is on foot through the Dungeness Wild-life Refuge. West of Sequim, at the junction of U.S. 101 and Kitchen Dick Lane, turn north and follow the refuge signs. The refuge is open daily, sunrise to sunset. There is a nominal entry fee, and do-nations are appreciated at the lighthouse. Allow ample time to hike the 5.5 miles (one way) from the refuge parking lot, and be aware of tide and weather conditions. Also, the lighthouse can be seen across Dungeness Bay from the Sequim Scenic Loop.

To become a "keeper for a week," contact (360) 683-9166. Or write to the USLS New Dungeness Chapter, P.O. Box 1283, Sequim, WA 98382-1283.

18. Smith Island Lighthouse

Most of the original lighthouse on Smith Island, near the east end of the Strait of Juan de Fuca, is gone. Built in 1858, the Cape Cod–style lighthouse stood on the island's west side, two hundred feet from the edge of a sand and clay bluff. The bluff gradually eroded, however, until the lighthouse had to be abandoned in 1957. Erosion continued, and in 1997 the last one-third of the lighthouse still clung precariously to the bluff's edge, fifty feet above the water.

When construction of the lighthouse first began, marauding Indian tribes from Southeast Alaska and British Columbia frequented the strait, and a blockhouse was built as living quarters for the workmen. No fighting occurred, and soon the dwelling with a forty-one-foot tower was completed. On October 18, 1858, a light was displayed from a fourth-order Fresnel lens. The blockhouse became the station's oil storage house.

The first principal keeper was Captain John Vail. He and his wife shared the dwelling with his assistant, Mr. Applegate. Soon after moving into the dwelling, the Vails were visited by their friend, James Swan. He was impressed by the Vails' four-acre garden and found the house "a model of neatness." He described Mrs. Vail as "a lady of taste . . . [who] during her lonely residence on the little island, made a beautiful collection of marine curiosities."

Shortly after Swan's visit, the quiet life on Smith Island was interrupted. Port Townsend residents, fearing attack by North Coast Indians from Canada, detained two northern chiefs. A few days later, the captain of a ship sailing in the strait saw five canoes headed for Smith Island. He altered course, picking up Vail, his wife, and

COAST GUARD MUSEUM NORTHWEST

Smith Island's Lighthouse hangs on to an eroding bluff.

their grandson to take them to Port Townsend. Applegate chose to remain at the lighthouse.

Volunteers from Port Townsend sailed to the island. Applegate signaled from the tower that all was quiet, and the ship returned to town. But that night the Indians landed on the island and fired at Applegate. He returned fire, wounding one, and the marauders retreated. The northern chiefs were released and sent to Victoria, British Columbia. With peace restored, the Vails resumed their post.

In 1860, Vail was replaced by Albert Milton, who in 1865 was replaced by John W. Bartlett. Seven years later C. P. Dyer became the keeper. One of Dyer's assistants, John Wellington, had worked at the station for only a couple of months when he drowned in 1880.

After Wellington's death, DeWitt C. Dennison became assistant keeper. He and his wife, Anna, came from Seattle with their six children. Dyer resigned a year later, and Dennison became principal keeper, a position that stayed in the family for the next twenty-five years. Anna served as her husband's assistant for one year, until her job was eliminated by the Lighthouse Service to cut costs.

During Dennison's time, peaceful North Coast Indians crossed the strait on their way to pick hops in Washington's Puyallup Valley. They often stopped overnight on the island. In July 1889 Dennison requested new hinges for the boathouse door, "in order to make the boathouse more secure as it is now time for the northern Indians to be coming along. . . . One canoe of Indians camped here last night."

Dennison suffered from an old wound that would not heal, and Frank, one of his three sons, often helped his ailing father. On October 27, 1891, the log read, "DeWitt Dennison, keeper of Smith Island Light Station, died and was taken to Whidbey Island and buried. Frank Dennison acting keeper." Three months later, Frank became principal keeper, but the rest of the Dennison family left soon after.

With his family gone, life was lonely for Frank. In June 1892 he asked the Lighthouse Service for a new sailboat, writing that "the boat now on hand is a very poor one. I use the boat here a great many more times than most of the other keepers as I have to go to Port Townsend and Whidbey Island in them most of the time."

A destination not mentioned in his request was Friday Harbor on San Juan Island, where Frank often sailed to court Fanny Larson. They were married in 1896, and two of their children, Winifred and DeWitt C. (also called "Dewey"), were born at the lighthouse.

When Dewey was older, he and his father would wade along the island's shore to collect flounder and crab from the shallows. One day while out walking, they were surprised to find a parrot. They assumed that it had flown from a passing ship. "It was tame, and we kept it quite awhile," said Dewey.

In 1905, Frank was transferred to the Fairway Island Lighthouse Station in Alaska. He left the Lighthouse Service in 1908 to fish and build boats, and two years later he was lost at sea in Alaskan waters.

During the 1930s, keeper Ray Dunson, hungry for fresh meat, raised rabbits on the island. He enjoyed rabbit stew and fried rabbit, but his furry livestock became a nuisance for future keepers. Sailors who operated a radio beacon on the island during World War II tried to exterminate the rabbits, without success. They asked the U.S. Fish and Wildlife Service for help. The biologists did what they could, but one resident commented, "The minute the [Wildlife Service] fellows pulled away in a boat, all you could see were pairs of ears sticking out of holes."

The bluff on which the lighthouse stood gradually eroded until, by 1949, its edge was only forty-five feet from the lighthouse. When the lighthouse was abandoned in 1957, a new light was placed on a steel tower near the center of the island. The Coast Guard keepers moved to frame houses built for Navy personnel.

When the light was automated in 1977, the Coast Guard keepers left. Today the island is closed to the public, but it is still the home of seabirds and rabbits.

19. Ediz Hook Lighthouse

Ediz Hook is a three-mile-long spit curving eastward into the Strait of Juan de Fuca, forming the harbor at Port Angeles. A light has shown from the end of the spit since the city was founded in 1862.

The first light was a bonfire in a grill mounted on a high tripod. Two lighthouses were later built, one in 1865, the other in 1908. They are gone, and today a light beams from a steel tower at the Coast Guard Air Station on the spit.

Credit for both the bonfire and the first lighthouse belongs to Victor Smith, the founder of Port Angeles. Smith, the new collector of customs for the Puget Sound District, arrived in Port Townsend from Washington, D.C., with his wife and three children in 1861. Smith's parents, brother, and sisters soon followed.

At the time Port Townsend was Washington Territory's port of entry, a role which brought maritime commerce to the fledgling town. But after Smith had been in town only a few months, he decided the port of entry should be moved to Port Angeles — even though only a few people lived along its timbered shores.

To discuss his plans with Congress and President Abraham Lincoln, Smith returned to Washington, D.C. Because of his lobbying efforts, Congress authorized moving the port of entry to Port Angeles. On June 19, 1862, President Lincoln signed an executive order setting aside 3,200 acres in Port Angeles for a military reservation, a customshouse, and a lighthouse at Ediz Hook.

Smith returned to Port Townsend in August. A near riot ensued as he took the records from the town's customshouse. The lighthouse tender *Shubrick*, then serving as a revenue cutter, trained its guns on the town to enforce Smith's orders. After Smith left for

Ediz Hook's 1865 lighthouse (foreground) was replaced by a lighthouse with a tower and fog signal (background) in 1908.

Port Angeles, angry Port Townsend residents hung him in effigy.

Until a lighthouse was built on Ediz Hook, Smith had the high tripod with grill placed on the spit to guide ships into the new port of entry. During the day, three men cut driftwood and piled it on the grill to burn through the night.

Victor, his wife, Caroline, and their four children, including a new baby, moved into a home near the new customshouse. In December 1863, while Smith was again in Washington, D.C., a flood of mud and debris crashed through the town destroying buildings, including the customshouse, where two employees were killed. The Smith home was damaged, but Caroline and the children survived. The disaster delayed work on the lighthouse.

In 1865 the bonfire beacon was replaced by the lighthouse, a two-story dwelling with a short tower projecting from one side of the roof. A light was displayed from a fifth-order Fresnel lens on April 2.

The principal keeper of the new lighthouse was George Smith, Victor's father. As the collector of customs, Victor appointed all lighthouse keepers, and this was the second time he had assigned his father to a keeper's position. In 1862, he had dismissed the principal keeper at the Cape Flattery Lighthouse and appointed his father. While the elder Smith was serving at Cape Flattery, a lighthouse inspector referred to him as "a peevish old man, under whose charges the lighthouse is rapidly going to destruction."

The Ediz Hook light had been lit only a few months when more tragedy struck. Returning on board a ship from another trip to Washington, D.C., Victor was drowned when the ship sank off the northern California coast. Then the Smiths' home burned. Caroline and the children moved to Ediz Hook to be near George Smith. Later she and her children moved to the Midwest. With Victor Smith gone and no opposition left, the port of entry was returned to Port Townsend in 1866.

George Smith retired in 1870, and his daughter Mary L. Smith, who had been assisting him for about a year, became principal keeper. Mary's appointment began a fifteen-year period when women served as principal keepers at the Ediz Hook Lighthouse.

Mary's sister Ella became her assistant in 1871, and served for nearly two years. When Ella left, seventeen-year-old Laura Balch became the assistant.

In 1874, Mary left Ediz Hook, seeking a warmer climate. She

became principal keeper at California's new Point Fermin Lighthouse near Los Angeles, where Ella joined her as the assistant keeper.

Laura Balch became principal keeper at Ediz Hook, where she was visited frequently by customs inspector Thomas Stratton. His visits turned into courtship, and they were married in 1876. The new Mrs. Stratton retained her position of principal keeper, and her husband became assistant keeper. Their two children were born at the lighthouse. Thomas died in 1885, and Laura and the children left the lighthouse a few months later.

The next year a fog bell was installed on the spit. The 3,000-pound bell, operated by clockwork machinery, was suspended from a large pyramidal tower on the northern edge of the spit, about 300 feet from the lighthouse.

The bell had been in place for a year when veteran lighthouse keeper Franklin Tucker arrived. By then the lighthouse had become a popular attraction. Visitors either walked the three miles along the spit or rowed across the harbor. On Sundays and special occasions, Tucker conducted tours, dressed in his brass-buttoned blue uniform. He retired in 1896.

In the meantime, mariners complained about the fog bell. Despite its size, it was "inaudible in some directions," reported the Lighthouse Board, noting, "It seems that some peculiarity occasions the trouble." So a new and stronger striking apparatus for the fog bell was installed.

This did not solve the problem, however, and in 1908 a second lighthouse was built at the station. Compressors for an air siren were installed in the fog signal building, and a new lens was placed in an attached thirty-five-foot tower. The old lighthouse, its tower removed, was converted to a dwelling, and another dwelling was built nearby.

Visitors and keepers continued to walk or row to the lighthouse station until Albert Beyer became keeper in 1916. During Beyer's sixteen years at Ediz Hook, he helped bring a road, electricity, and city water to the station.

The fog bell on its pyramidal tower operated until the new Ediz Hook Lighthouse was completed in 1908.

Chris C. Waters was the principal keeper in 1939, when the original lighthouse was torn down. He was still keeper when, in 1946, the station's second lighthouse was removed because it had become a hazard to aircraft at the Coast Guard Air Station. The 1908 structure was sold and barged across the harbor. Today this lighthouse—minus the tower—is a private residence at the corner of Fourth and Albert Streets in Port Angeles. With the second lighthouse gone, the modern optic atop the air station's control tower has become the last reminder of Ediz Hook's early lights.

One hundred years after Port Townsend citizens hung Victor Smith in effigy, Port Angeles citizens honored him. During the city's centennial in 1962, the Daughters of the American Revolution placed an historical marker at the Clallam County Courthouse, commemorating Smith as the founder of Port Angeles.

The Slip Point Lighthouse, the last built on the Strait of Juan de Fuca, fell victim to landslides and was dismantled in the 1950s.

20. Slip Point Lighthouse

The Slip Point Lighthouse, the fourth lighthouse built on the Strait of Juan de Fuca, began operation in 1905. It was located at the base of a steep hillside at the eastern entrance to Clallam Bay, at a point named by an early Clallam postmaster. He described it as "a very broken up formation [where] slides frequently occur." True to its name, the point gradually slipped until the lighthouse had to be abandoned.

Long before the construction of the lighthouse, a landslide on the point served as a natural landmark for mariners. It was often obscured by fog or smoke from forest fires, and though the lighthouses at Cape Flattery and Ediz Hook had fog signals, there were none in the sixty-five miles separating them.

In the 1880s many ships sailed the strait, including small steamers stopping at towns along the way to pick up passengers and freight. Ship captains and owners wanted a fog signal between Cape Flattery and Ediz Hook, and in 1897 the Lighthouse Board requested funds for one at Slip Point. Three years later they included a light in their request and received $12,500.

The Lighthouse Service hired local labor to build a fog signal building to house a Daboll trumpet; a lens lantern was installed on top. In March 1905 principal keeper Hans Score and his assistant, Sam Morris, moved into a comfortable two-story duplex dwelling in an open swale near the bay. They lit the light on April 1. To tend the light and fog signal, the keepers walked a long catwalk built on pilings over the rocky shore. At high tide, waves crashed beneath their feet.

Mariners welcomed the new fog signal, but one night when it

97

was most needed, it was silent. In late afternoon on January 11, 1907, the steamer *Alice Gertrude* left a Clallam Bay dock and headed west for Neah Bay. The sky was filled with thick gray clouds and snow began to fall, blown by fierce winds. For two hours the ship struggled against the wind and waves but hardly moved.

Captain Charles Kallstrom ordered the helmsman to turn the ship back to Clallam Bay. Two men stood on the bow, snow hitting their faces as they listened for the Slip Point fog signal. They heard nothing, but the captain saw a light. Since no fog signal could be heard coming from that direction, the captain assumed the light was the lantern on the dock. As he steered toward it, the ship slammed onto a rocky reef and was pinned by pounding waves. Feeling it safer to remain on board, Captain Kallstrom gathered the passengers in the lounge, where they huddled in blankets.

A keeper at the Cape Flattery Lighthouse received an urgent telegraph message to send rescue boats. According to the lighthouse log, he "rang up the village [Neah Bay] got Washburn. I told him to send a canoe to inform the *Wyadda* with most possible haste." The tugboats *Wyadda* and *Lorne* left immediately, towing Makah canoes to rescue the passengers.

The rescue was too dangerous to attempt in the storm and darkness, so the tugs stood by until daybreak. All aboard were saved, but the *Alice Gertrude* was a total loss.

It is unclear why the fog signal was silent. One record stated it was turned off for repairs; another claims it was turned off because the *Alice Gertrude* had left, and no more vessels were scheduled to arrive at Clallam Bay that night.

In 1916 a new fog signal was installed, and a tower was added to the fog signal building. The lens lantern was replaced by a fourth-order Fresnel lens.

Dorothy Zauner Armstrong remembers the fog signal building. As a girl, Dorothy and her two younger sisters spent the summer of 1927 at Slip Point. Her uncle, Carl Lien, was the principal keeper, and her aunt substituted for the assistant keeper when he was on vacation. Dorothy, her cousin, and her aunt often played cards in the fog signal building from 8 p.m. to midnight, while her aunt took the keeper's watch.

Dorothy also remembers many stuffed birds being kept upstairs in the dwelling. Lien's off-duty hours were spent as a taxidermist for the University of Washington.

In the 1950s the lighthouse was dismantled. It was replaced by an unmanned light and fog signal on a pile structure near the point, which were still reached via the catwalk. The dwelling was occupied by the Clallam County Sheriff Department and Coast Guard personnel stationed at Neah Bay.

GARY LENTZ

In the 1920s Carl Lien served as lightkeeper at Slip Point.

———

Yet the point continued to experience landslides. In the winter of 1996-1997, a section of the catwalk was lost to a slide, and the light and fog signal were threatened by new slides. The Coast Guard moved the light and fog signal about twelve miles east, and the keepers' dwelling was abandoned.

Today mariners will note only a landslide-scarred point that marks the site where the Slip Point Lighthouse once stood.

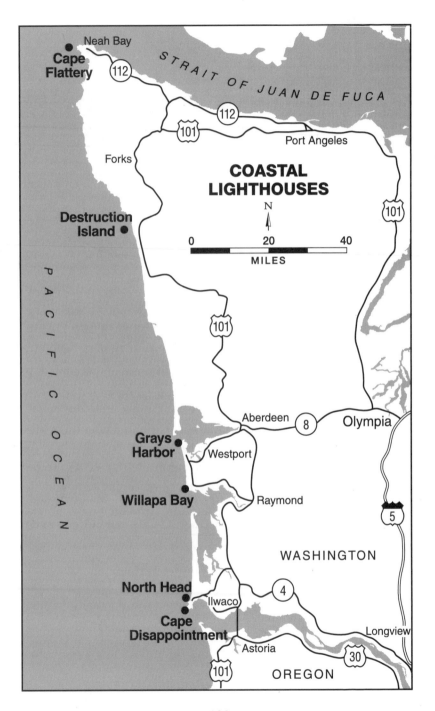

Neah Bay

Cape Flattery

(112)

STRAIT OF JUAN DE FUCA

(112)

(101)

Port Angeles

Forks

COASTAL LIGHTHOUSES

N

0   20   40

MILES

(101)

Destruction Island

P A C I F I C   O C E A N

(101)

Aberdeen (8) Olympia

Grays Harbor

Westport

Willapa Bay

Raymond

(5)

WASHINGTON

North Head

Ilwaco

(4)

Cape Disappointment

Longview

Astoria

(30)

(101) OREGON

COASTAL SENTRIES

Washington's coast extends 138 miles from Cape Disappointment, at the mouth of the Columbia River, to Cape Flattery, at the entrance to the Strait of Juan de Fuca.

Spanish explorers began sailing along the coast in 1774. The British and French followed, searching for the fabled Northwest Passage. The passage did not exist, but Britain's first voyage, in 1788, started the Northwest trade in sea otter pelts. By 1790, many fur trading vessels were sailing the coast.

Seafarers found the coastal waters and weather treacherous. Fierce waves often crashed across the Columbia River bar. Shoals shifted in shallow bays, and offshore rocks and islets added to the danger. Winter gales were common, with heavy rain and sometimes snow, while summer fogs reduced visibility.

Starting with California's gold rush of 1849, ships from San Francisco began to sail up the Columbia to take on cargoes of lumber, grain, and produce. Some entered Willapa Bay for cargoes of oysters, while others continued north to round Cape Flattery on their way to sawmills along Puget Sound. More ships followed as the region's economy grew.

Washington's first lighthouse was established at Cape Disappointment in 1856. Two years later there were lighthouses at Willapa Bay and on Tatoosh Island near Cape Flattery. The last three lighthouses along the coast, at North Head, Grays Harbor, and Destruction Island, were completed by 1898.

The Cape Disappointment Lighthouse, the oldest lighthouse in Washington, has guided mariners since 1856.

21. Cape Disappointment Lighthouse

The Cape Disappointment Lighthouse is the oldest in Washington. Still operating, it has guided ships along the coast and across the Columbia River bar since 1856.

The idea of building a lighthouse on Cape Disappointment was first mentioned in the 1848 act creating Oregon Territory, which included present-day Washington. The act made provision for "the construction of lighthouses at Cape Disappointment and New Dunginess [sic]. . . . " At the time there were no lighthouses on the West Coast, and Cape Disappointment was a logical place for one.

The cape, a headland on the north side of the Columbia River's mouth, was named by British fur trader John Meares. In 1788 he was looking for a great river described by a Spanish sea explorer. Unable to find the river, Meares named the headland Cape Disappointment.

Four years later, Boston fur trader Captain Robert Gray found the river and named it for his ship, *Columbia Rediviva*. Despite its treacherous bar, the Columbia River soon became an important waterway for Americans and British engaged in the fur trade.

The first known beacon on Cape Disappointment in 1812 assisted the American ship *Beaver*, which was bringing supplies to Fort Astor, now Astoria, Oregon. For several days the ship lay off the Columbia's entrance, waiting for favorable conditions at the bar. To assist the ship, men from the fort rowed twelve miles across the river and climbed to the top of the headland. They hoisted a white flag and at night set fire to trees, "to serve in lieu of a lighthouse," wrote one.

In the 1840s, three trees near the cape's crest were topped.

Captains took their bearings from the cut trees and steered for the cape's southerly tip to sail through the deepest waters at the river's mouth.

Vessel traffic on the Columbia River increased during the California gold rush; in 1850, 160 ships crossed the river's bar. A lighthouse was urgently needed on the cape and at other sites on the West Coast. The U.S. Coast Survey was assigned to decide where the first should be built. By 1852 the Lighthouse Board had received appropriations to build lighthouses at eight of the selected locations, from California's Point Loma to Cape Disappointment.

In 1853 the bark *Oriole* arrived off the Columbia's mouth, carrying construction materials and workmen to build the cape's lighthouse, but the ship sank as it crossed the bar. Its crew and workmen survived, but the materials were lost. The next year new supplies were delivered, and lighthouse construction began.

When completed, the cone-shaped tower on the cape stood fifty-three feet tall. Its brick walls were five feet thick at the base and two feet thick at the top. Then came another delay. A new lighting system using Fresnel lenses had been ordered *after* the tower was already designed. So the tower was too small to hold the first-order lens, and it had to be rebuilt — which took two more years.

On October 15, 1856, the lamp was finally lit, shining a fixed-white light across the bar and out to sea. The lamp had five wicks that formed a circle eighteen inches in diameter. It consumed 170 gallons of whale oil a month. To drain condensation from the lantern, grooves in its ceiling led water out through eagle-head gargoyles, which can still be seen beneath the eaves of the lantern's roof.

In front of the tower, a 1,600-pound fog bell hung outside a frame building that housed its striking mechanism. In foggy weather the bell was struck nine blows every minute.

The keepers' house, now gone, was about a quarter of a mile from the tower on the leeward side of the headland. In 1860 keeper

John Boyd lived in the one-and-one-half-story dwelling with his wife and infant son, and two assistant keepers, including seventeen-year-old George Easterbrook.

The young keeper's grit was tested one winter night as he labored up the hill in pouring rain to the lighthouse for his pre-dawn watch. A gust of wind nearly blew Easterbrook off the narrow ridge trail, and he crawled the rest of the way to the tower, then climbed the spiral staircase.

After refueling the lamp, he went outside to clean salt spray from the windows. As he started to work, the lantern room door,

An artillery officer, circa 1880, stands near the cannon set up on Cape Disappointment during the Civil War.

———

which had a broken latch, slammed shut. He couldn't pry it open and didn't know how to get back inside. Frightened but keeping his duties in mind, he wiped the glass until he was soaked and cold.

Then he began to worry about the light going out — and about not being paid if he didn't do his job. Seeing the lightning rod, a long copper-wire rope suspended from the roof, he grabbed it and began to slide down the tower. A gust of wind "caught me . . . and swung me out over the depths," he later wrote. When he swung back, he hugged the tower, dropped to the ground, and passed out. Cold rain on his face soon woke him. He crawled through the tower's door and finished his watch. Easterbrook quit the Lighthouse Service a few months later, and eventually he became a doctor.

During the Civil War, a fort (later named Fort Canby) was established on Cape Disappointment. Union cannon were set up along the ridge next to the lighthouse and pointed at the river's entrance. In 1871, after vibrations from practice firing shattered the original fog bell house, a new one was built. Mariners, however, had long complained that the signal was inaudible from its height, so the bell was discontinued. Other types of fog signals also proved ineffective, and the light station remained without one. Later, the bell was used at the West Point Lighthouse, then at the Warrior Rock Lighthouse on the Columbia. It is now displayed in front of the courthouse in St. Helens, Oregon.

The same year that the new fog bell house was built, the keepers, including principal keeper Joel Munson, moved into a second dwelling. After Munson had arrived at Cape Disappointment in 1865, he became distressed at the increasing number of shipwrecks at the river's entrance. Salvaging a small boat from one shipwreck, he made it into a lifesaving boat. Munson and volunteers used it to rescue survivors from two ships wrecked on the south side of the river's bar. Munson's efforts led to the establishment of government lifesaving stations at Fort Canby and at North Cove near the Willapa Bay Lighthouse in 1877.

Principal keeper Al Harris was serving as captain of the Fort Canby Life-Saving Station in 1881, when a watchman in front of the lighthouse tower spotted a vessel in distress. The watchman fired a small cannon to signal the station, and Harris and his men responded, rescuing nineteen people. Three years later, they rescued 175 passengers of the *Queen of the Pacific,* which went aground on Clatsop Beach, Oregon. Today the Coast Guard Station at Cape Disappointment serves as the lifesaving station.

After forty-two years of shining from the Cape Disappointment tower, the first-order lens was moved to the North Head Lighthouse, which was being built two miles north on the cape. A new fourth-order Fresnel lens installed at Cape Disappointment displayed alternating red and white flashes.

When war was declared in December 1941, the lights at the

Columbia's entrance were extinguished as part of a blackout along the Pacific Coast. On December 10 a distress call was heard from the ship SS *Mauna Ala*. Carrying Christmas trees bound for Honolulu, the ship had been ordered to return to the mainland. The captain, unaware of the blackout, ran the ship aground south of the river's entrance. All aboard were saved, but the ship and cargo were lost. After this accident, the Columbia River lights were relit.

Later Cape Disappointment's light was nearly extinguished permanently. In 1965, the Coast Guard reported that the Columbia River "is adequately marked by the Columbia River lightship and entrance range lights." Mariners protested so much, however, that the light remained lit.

The fourth-order lens placed in the tower in 1898 still guides mariners today. From a small Coast Guard observation station in front of the tower, the person on watch observes bar conditions, logs vessels leaving and entering, and handles communications during rescues.

The Washington State Parks and Recreation Commission is negotiating the transfer of the tower to Fort Canby State Park, a process that takes several years. Inside the park is the Lewis and Clark Interpretive Center, which includes displays of the first-order Fresnel lens installed at Cape Disappointment in 1856 and later used at North Head, and equipment used by the Life-Saving Service.

Directions and Hours

From downtown Ilwaco, follow the signs to Fort Canby State Park. The interpretive center, staffed by volunteers, is open year-round, 10-5. Closed Christmas Day. For current information, phone Fort Canby State Park, (360) 642-3078.

Pending transfer of the tower, there are no tours of the Cape Disappointment Lighthouse, but it can be seen from the outside. A road in the park leads to the Coast Guard station, where parking is available. A 1.5-mile-long trail leads uphill to the tower's base.

Two miles from the Cape Disappointment Lighthouse, the 1898 North Head tower guides mariners coming from the north.

22. North Head Lighthouse

Established in 1898, the North Head Lighthouse is just two miles north of the Cape Disappointment Lighthouse on the bold, tree-covered cape. For many years it appeared that the 1856 Cape Disappointment Lighthouse would be sufficient to mark the headland and nearby coastal waters. However, the 1869 *Coast Pilot* noted that "Vessels coming from the northward cannot see the [Cape Disappointment] light until nearly in the latitude of the [Columbia] river."

As coastal traffic increased, many shipwrecks occurred on the beaches north of the cape. In 1882 *Harvest Home*, bound for Port Townsend in heavy fog, drifted ashore. The crew was not aware that they were so close to the beach until they heard roosters crowing in a nearby barn. At low tide, the captain and crew walked ashore. Local residents salvaged wagons from the ship's cargo, and its hull slowly rotted in the sand. The American bark *Whistler* in 1883, the ship *Carrie B. Lake* in 1886, and the barkentine *Grace Roberts* in 1887 were all wrecked in the same area.

In 1889, the Lighthouse Board agreed that "the present light at Cape Disappointment is inadequate for purposes of commerce and navigation." They proposed moving Cape Disappointment's first-order Fresnel lens to a new lighthouse at North Head. With this new station and the proposed lighthouses at Grays Harbor and Destruction Island, the board noted, the north coast would be well marked with first-order lights from Oregon's Tillamook Head to Washington's Cape Flattery.

Construction at North Head began in 1896. The sixty-five-foot tower, standing on the edge of a 130-foot-high cliff, was built with a sandstone base and thick brick walls. A plaster overlay was painted white. Two large keepers' dwellings, a barn, and a chicken coop were built on a rise above the lighthouse.

When the tower was completed, Cape Disappointment's first-order lens was disassembled and moved to North Head. Workmen reassembled each section of the four-ton lens by matching numbers stamped in the brass frames. A fourth-order Fresnel lens was installed at Cape Disappointment. On May 16, 1898, the North Head Lighthouse displayed its first light.

Since the two lighthouses were only two miles apart, their light characteristics had to be distinctly different. North Head displayed a fixed-white light, while Cape Disappointment showed alternating red and white flashes.

Keepers entered the new tower through a small workroom, which helped maintain a dry interior in the tower and provided office space for the keepers. Its floor edged with mosaic tile, the workroom had a desk against one wall and a wood-burning stove in a corner. The room is still intact and serves as an example of the workrooms at other coastal towers.

Sixty-nine numbered steps spiraled up the inside of the tower to the lantern, which was made of quarter-inch-thick glass edged in metal. Outside, a balcony circled the lantern. Hand grips protruded from the window frames so keepers could hang on while cleaning the glass on windy days. They used the grips most of the time, as North Head is reportedly the third windiest location in the nation.

Wind and weather conditions at the cape had been recorded since 1864, first by soldiers stationed there, then by the U.S. Signal Corps. In 1902 the U.S. Weather Bureau built a station at North Head between the tower and the keepers' dwellings. The strongest winds, recorded on January 29, 1921, were clocked at 126 miles per hour before the instrument blew away. Though the weather station's houses were anchored by steel rods embedded in concrete, the residents left during the storm and took refuge in the sturdier assistant keepers' home.

The Lighthouse Service reported that other Washington lighthouses were damaged by this same storm. At Willapa Bay the woodshed was blown down, and at Cape Flattery a dwelling's chimney was blown over and the flagpole was lifted from the ground.

Early keepers at North Head included Mabel E. Bretherton. She was transferred to North Head in 1905 after serving for two years at Oregon's Cape Blanco Lighthouse. Two years after arriving at North Head, Mabel resigned from the Lighthouse Service.

Frank C. Hammond was second assistant keeper in 1923 when the principal keeper's wife fell off the cliff. Hammond was commended by the Lighthouse Service for recovering "at extreme personal risk, the body of the wife of the keeper at this station."

In 1935 the first-order Fresnel lens that had shone from the cape's two lighthouses for a total of nearly eighty years was retired. Electricity was installed at North Head, and the first-order lens was replaced by a fourth-order Fresnel lens. The original lens is now at the Lewis and Clark Interpretive Center at Fort Canby State Park.

The Coast Guard had been in charge at North Head and Cape Disappointment for about two years when it was faced with a unique emergency. Shortly after the start of World War II, according to the log, on June 22, 1942, at 12:35 a.m. the keepers of the two lighthouses were ordered to extinguish the lights.

A Japanese submarine had fired on Fort Stevens, on the Oregon side of the Columbia River. No damage occurred, and soldiers did not return the fire, reportedly because they did not want to disclose their location. The lights were turned on when the danger was over.

The 1950s brought change to North Head. The weather station closed, and two aero beacons replaced the fourth-order lens. It is now on display at the Columbia River Maritime Museum in Astoria, Oregon.

The lighthouse was automated in 1961, and Coast Guard personnel were reassigned. The aero beacons are still inside the lantern, but the operative light is a modern optic mounted on the tower's gallery.

Neither North Head nor Cape Disappointment has a fog signal. The stations' great height and the crashing waves on the cape below create dead spots, making a fog signal inaudible to mariners.

As with the Cape Disappointment tower, the Washington State Parks and Recreation Commission is negotiating with the Coast Guard to transfer the North Head tower to Fort Canby State Park. Meanwhile, the park is licensed to conduct tours of the tower.

The two keepers' dwellings have long been part of the park; the assistants' dwelling, a duplex, is occupied by park personnel. In 1997, the single family keepers' dwelling near the tower was renovated under the direction of park ranger Evan Roberts.

Donated labor and supplies made it possible for the dwelling to be made ready for visitors. Furnished quarters, which include linens and utensils, can comfortably accommodate up to six people. Minimum stays are for two nights, or three on holiday weekends. In 199, the dwelling could be rented for $200 per night, plus tax. Revenues are used for renovating other historic residences in the park.

Directions and Hours

Follow the signs for Fort Canby State Park from downtown Ilwaco. A short, signed road leads off the park's loop to a parking area near the dwellings and a path to the North Head Lighthouse.

Lighthouse tours, at one dollar per person, are subject to the availability of volunteers, but are usually held daily in the summertime from 10-6. For tour information or for reservations at the keeper's dwelling, call Fort Canby State Park at (360) 642-3078.

23. Willapa Bay Lighthouse

This lighthouse, built in 1858 on the north side of the entrance to today's Willapa Bay, was for many years called the Shoalwater Bay Lighthouse. Battered by currents and waves, the lighthouse and the point where it stood were washed away over fifty years ago.

The bay lies about twenty-eight miles north of the Columbia River and was first named by John Meares, a British fur trader. While exploring the coast in July 1788, Meares saw what appeared to be an entrance to a broad sound. Steering toward the opening, "we shoaled our water gradually to six fathoms," he wrote in his log. On seeing breakers roll across the bay's shallows, he turned his ship about and left behind the name Shoalwater Bay.

Years later Lieutenant Commander James Alden, aboard the ship *Active* on a surveying trip for the United States, reported that Shoalwater Bay was "full of shoals, as its name implies, but there is plenty of water among them, and they are generally bare at low water."

Shoalwater Bay had become an important coastal harbor even before Washington became a territory in 1853. The bay was rich with oysters, and ships loaded with the delectable shellfish sailed regularly for San Francisco.

James Swan, an early pioneer and historian, was one of the bay's oystermen who recognized the need for a lighthouse at the entrance. One day in 1855 Swan sat on a log along the shore with J. Patton Anderson, a congressional candidate for Washington Territory. "What do you boys want down here on Shoalwater Bay?" asked Anderson. "We want a lighthouse," replied Swan, "and we want the bay surveyed and buoyed out."

Neither was aware that the Lighthouse Board had already received congressional authorization for a lighthouse on the bay, as well as for lighthouses at Cape Flattery, New Dungeness, and Smith Island.

Construction of the lighthouse on a low, sandy bluff began early in 1858. It was a Cape Cod–style masonry building, with a forty-two-foot circular tower rising through the roof, on a base of New England marble. The marble had been delivered by sailing ship and lightered to shore in Native American canoes. The light was first displayed from a fourth-order Fresnel lens on October 1, 1858.

The first principal keeper was Captain Wells, assisted by Daniel Wilson. After operating for less than a year the lighthouse was closed, possibly because its remote location made lamp fuel difficult to deliver.

The lighthouse reopened in July 1861, with Robert H. Espy as principal keeper. Espy was one of the first settlers on Shoalwater Bay. He and his friend I. A. Clark had come in 1854 to harvest oysters. They built a cabin on the west side of the bay and called their new home Oysterville. Espy had been in the oyster business for seven years before becoming the lighthouse keeper. Perhaps oysters suited him better, for he served at the lighthouse less than a year.

In the mid-1860s the lighthouse again was threatened with closure. Vessel traffic into Shoalwater Bay waned, and the Lighthouse Board considered extinguishing the light. A district inspector, however, reported that "The commerce using that light has somewhat increased during the past year, and promises to still further increase hereafter."

Erosion at the point became evident in the late 1860s. A bulkhead was built to protect the lighthouse's foundation, and the ground surrounding the structure was covered with planks to lessen the amount of sand blowing into the lighthouse.

By 1877 numerous shipwrecks had occurred along the Washington coast. To reduce the loss of lives, lifesaving stations

COAST GUARD MUSEUM NORTHWEST

**At Willapa Bay the lighthouse grounds were covered with planks
to keep sand from blowing into the building.**

were established, with one called North Cove located near the
lighthouse. Initially, each lifesaving station was run by one person,
assisted by volunteers.

Like the lighthouse, the North Cove Life-Saving Station was
remote, and volunteers were sorely needed on October 31, 1881.
The master of the bark *Lammerlaw* mistook Shoalwater Bay for the
Columbia River, and the ship drove aground in a storm near
Leadbetter Point, at the bay's south entrance. Albert T. Stream, captain of the lifesaving station, saw the ship in distress, but no
volunteers were nearby to mount a rescue.

At the time, Sidney Smith was principal keeper at the lighthouse. According to Lucile McDonald in her book, *Coast Country*, keeper Smith hiked fifteen miles to recruit assistance. While Smith was gone, Stream built signal fires in the dunes to let the crew know help was coming. The fifteen men clung to the ship's rigging as waves crashed against the ship's hull.

Thirty-six hours later, volunteers finally arrived. They were local Coast Indians, who manned the oars while Stream took the helm, and women missionaries, who pushed the boat into the turbulent waters. The ship's crew was rescued, and Stream received a gold life-saving medal for his efforts.

Although keeper Smith served at the lighthouse for about three years, turnover of assistant keepers was frequent. In October 1880, Smith wrote in the log, "Mr. John Gelbin was placed on duty as Assistant Keeper. Goodbye Mitchell, you infernal thief and Bummer." At the end of July 1883, Smith wrote, "This will be my last full month at this station, thank the Lord."

The name Shoalwater Bay prevailed until the 1890s. Local citizens felt the name was a commercial handicap, and changed the name to Willapa, after the local Willapa Indians. A sea captain confirmed this belief, saying, "Shipmasters used to be afraid of this harbor because of the old name. . . ."

Though keeper Smith seemed to have no regrets about leaving, Olaf Hansen found the station to his liking. Hansen transferred from Oregon's Heceta Head Lighthouse to Willapa Bay in 1920. He, his wife, and their six children rode in a wagon from Heceta Head to Florence, Oregon, where they boarded the lighthouse tender *Rose* for the trip to Willapa Bay. Hansen stayed at the Willapa Bay station for ten years, then retired after being with the Lighthouse Service for thirty-six years.

Meanwhile, the point's sandy bluffs continued to erode. On December 24, 1940, the *Tacoma News Tribune* reported that an eighty-five-mile-per-hour hurricane had lashed at the lighthouse and its foundation. The article stated that the Coast Guard removed the furniture, "the musty records, the fine French glass reflectors [Fresnel lens] used since 1858, and the brass light fittings."

On December 26 the newspaper reported that the entire south wall of the lighthouse collapsed, "undermined by a high tide and heavy surf, . . . and a temporary light was set up about a quarter mile inland."

Since then, the Coast Guard has built more towers with lights, each one placed farther inland as the point continued to wear away. Today the automated Willapa Light is three-quarters of a mile from where the lighthouse once stood. Like other coastal lights, it is maintained by the Coast Guard Aids to Navigation Team Astoria, Oregon.

The Grays Harbor Lighthouse was the last of six lighthouses built on Washington's coast.

24. Grays Harbor Lighthouse

Grays Harbor has the tallest lighthouse in Washington. Standing near sea level, the 107-foot-tall octagonal tower rises high above the surrounding sand dunes and trees. Often called the "Westport Lighthouse" by local residents, it has marked the harbor's entrance since 1898.

With sawmills at Aberdeen, Hoquiam, and Cosmopolis, Grays Harbor became a major lumber shipping center in the early 1880s. In 1884 Congress appropriated $15,500 for a small harbor light at the bay's entrance. Point Brown on the north and Point Chehalis on the south were considered.

In 1887, the Lighthouse Board decided a harbor light would not be adequate to "meet the demands of the commerce and navigation of this part of the coast." So the board requested an additional $60,000 to establish a seacoast tower and light at the harbor's entrance. This additional funding was received from Congress in 1895.

Point Chehalis was selected for the station, and construction began in 1897. A road was built to the point to transport materials by wagon. Soon two dwellings, one for the principal keeper and a duplex for the assistants, stood east of the brick tower. A large fog signal building stood on the seaward side. But delivery of the tower's metalwork was delayed, and it was not completed until 1898.

Inside the dimly lit tower, 135 metal stairs, bolted to the walls, spiraled up to the lantern room that enclosed a third-order Fresnel lens, built in 1895 by Henry LePaute and Sons in Paris. Floating in a twenty-gallon pool of mercury, the lens was turned by a clockwork mechanism, with a large weight that hung down inside the tower. Showing flashes of red and white, the light was commissioned on June 30, 1898.

Like the tower's metalwork, the fog signals were late in arriving — they did not begin operation until March 1899. Two steam-powered sirens, with trumpets projecting seaward, were activated by a coal-fired boiler. A windmill near the building pumped well water to the boiler.

The new station was built close to the ocean beach. Unlike many areas along the southern Washington coast that fell victim to erosion, these shores experienced accretion over time. The lighthouse is now nearly one-half mile from the pounding surf.

The first principal keeper was Christian Zauner, who arrived from Destruction Island with his wife, Hermine, and two young daughters. Zauner's journals and records, provided by his grand-daughter, Dorothy Zauner Armstrong, offer revealing glimpses of life at the lighthouse.

In February 1900 Zauner requested from the Lighthouse Service "Sunday visiting hours on afternoon only as the Excursion Boats do not arrive until about noon." He also wrote that visitors should not be admitted on foggy or rainy days, because "too much wet sand and moisture [is] carried up into the lens room."

The next month Zauner wrote that the fog signal boiler was "not in good condition. . . . It requires one's whole attention to keep steam pressure up to the notch. . . . It requires nearly 200 pounds of coal per hour of fog."

Zauner's problems with the fog signal were resolved in 1916, when its building burned down and a new oil-fired signal was established closer to the ocean. Today the fog signal is on a jetty northwest of the lighthouse.

When Dorothy was a child, her family lived in Westport and she often visited her grandfather. She remembered climbing the many stairs and seeing the heavy clockwork weight hanging in the tower. By watching the weight, "Papa Chris told me he could tell when an earthquake had occurred somewhere in the world," she said. One day in September 1923, Zauner was climbing the tower stairs when

Grays Harbor's lighthouse and fog signal building were much closer to the shore before sand accretion took place.

the weight began to swing violently. An area near Tokyo, Japan, was being struck by an earthquake that would kill 140,000 people.

On July 31, 1925, Zauner turned the station's keys over to J. Wilson, and wrote that he "removed from watch room desk personal spyglasses." After attending a surprise party in honor of his retirement that evening, he and Hermine settled into their home a few blocks from the station.

A new principal keeper, Arvel Settles, arrived with his wife, Helga, and their five children the following year. Settles had entered the Lighthouse Service in 1920, and had served at various California and Oregon lighthouses before coming to Grays Harbor.

The family lived in the large, spacious single-family dwelling. With many children to feed, Mrs. Settles kept the pantry well stocked.

Once a month the family went shopping in Aberdeen. Their son Charles recalled, "There was always a full ham hanging in the pantry, a slab of bacon, and a case of eggs."

As in keeper Zauner's time, many people were intrigued by lighthouses and came to see the one at Grays Harbor. During visiting hours, Settles and the assistant keepers dressed in their uniforms to escort visitors up and down the stairs of the tall tower. They often grew weary and were happy when visiting hours were over, Helga said.

In 1935 Settles was transferred to the Lime Kiln Lighthouse on San Juan Island, and his assistant, Roy "Sharkey" Jacobsen, became principal keeper. When the Coast Guard took over, Jacobsen became a coast guardsman and remained at Grays Harbor until he retired in 1945.

Coast Guard keepers stayed at the lighthouse until the late 1960s, when the original lens, then turned by an electric motor, and the fog signal were automated. The old dwellings have been removed.

In the early 1990s, health concerns caused the Coast Guard to remove the mercury from the base of the lens. Curtains were drawn around the then-stationary lens to protect it from the sun. A small, modern optic, flashing red and white, was installed outside on the lantern room gallery.

In 1998 the Westport–South Beach Historical Society negotiated a lease agreement with the Coast Guard and began planning for regularly scheduled tours of the lighthouse.

The historical society also operates the Westport Maritime Museum, housed in a 1939 building that was once a Coast Guard Lifeboat Station. Exhibits include old photographs of the Willapa Bay and Grays Harbor light stations, and lighthouse and lifesaving equipment.

In a more ambitious project, the historical society raised $150,000 in donations to construct a new building on the museum grounds to house the first-order Fresnel lens from the Destruction

Island Lighthouse. The building, dedicated in the fall of 1998, is designed to give visitors a dramatic view of the massive lens and its pedestal.

Directions and Hours

The Grays Harbor Lighthouse can be seen from a viewing platform on Ocean Avenue in Westport. For tour schedules, call the Westport Maritime Museum at (360) 268-0078.

The museum is at 2201 West Haven Drive, Westport. It's open daily, Memorial Day weekend through Labor Day, 10-5. The rest of the year, Wed. to Fri., 12-4; Sat. and Sun., 10-5.

The Destruction Island Lighthouse before its first-order Fresnel lens was replaced by a modern optic in 1995.

25. Destruction Island Lighthouse

"Isolated, forlorn, and barren," was one coast guardsman's description of Destruction Island. The small, flat-topped island rises about fifty feet above the water. Rock outcrops spread from its shores like tentacles. The mainland, only three miles away, is uninhabited except for traffic along U.S. Highway 101. The nearest town is La Push, twenty miles to the north.

The island was named for two tragedies. In 1775 Spanish sailors rowed ashore near the island to fill their water casks. They were killed by Coast Indians, and the Spanish named the island *Isla de Dolores*, or "Island of Sorrows." Twelve years later, sailors from a British ship rowed up a nearby river to obtain water, and they met the same fate. The ship's captain, Charles W. Barkley, named the river Destruction. Eventually, the river's name was changed to Hoh, and the island was called Destruction.

Though the island was reserved for lighthouse purposes in 1866, it was not until almost twenty years later that the Lighthouse Board requested $85,000 "for the establishment of a first class light and fog signal." But Congress appropriated only $45,000. The board persisted, and the following year Congress appropriated the full amount.

In August 1888, a boat landing was built in a small cove on the island's east side. A derrick was installed to lift supplies and materials from boats, and a tramway was laid from the landing to the island's top.

By 1889 much of the station was finished, including two dwellings, a barn, and the fog signal building housing boilers and duplicate sirens. Work on the tower had not begun, however, pending another $10,000 from Congress.

On August 26, 1889, Christian Zauner, then assistant keeper at

Oregon's Tillamook Rock Lighthouse, was directed to assume duty as keeper of the Destruction Island station. The lighthouse inspector instructed Zauner, "familiarize yourself with the fog signal machinery, assist in getting it in place, and when ready for operation take charge of it." Zauner, who was single, arrived on August 29, and assistant Thomas Campbell and his wife arrived later.

Meanwhile, Congress approved more funding, and construction of the ninety-four-foot tower began in October 1890. Brick by brick, the tower slowly took shape. It was six feet wide at the base and four feet wide at the top. Coast Indians who watched the construction later remembered the "difficulty landing the stones" used in the tower. Upon completion, the tower was sheathed in iron.

After months of preparation, on January 1, 1892, Zauner wrote in his journal, "Lit the lamp at 4:26 p.m. for the first time, to guide mariners. Keeper on first watch." As the first-order Fresnel lens rotated, turned by a clockwork mechanism, its twenty-four "bullseye" panels cast a flashing light to a distance of over twenty miles.

While at Destruction Island, Zauner married a widow named Hermine, who had a five-year-old daughter. The couple later had a daughter, Mabel, born in 1895.

Mabel's daughter, Dorothy Zauner Armstrong, recalled being told by her grandmother how they, like later island keepers, kept a cow, chickens, and a vegetable garden. "Hoh Indians came to the island in large, oceangoing canoes to trade woven mats and baskets for flour and sugar," Dorothy said. "They would sit on the kitchen floor and watch my grandma bathe my mother in a large, tin washtub."

In 1898 Zauner was transferred to the Grays Harbor Lighthouse. Mark Grayson, who had been Zauner's assistant for six years, became principal keeper. He and his family stayed at Destruction Island for seven more years.

Once the Coast Guard took over the lighthouse, five to eight men were assigned to the station; their families stayed on the mainland. Considered isolation duty, the assignments were for eighteen months. Each man worked for six weeks and then received two and a half weeks of shore leave. Every three weeks, supplies and mail were delivered by a Coast Guard motor launch.

In 1963, the Coast Guard announced its intention to abandon the station. The light and fog signal were to be replaced by lighted buoys with sound signals near the island and new lights on the mainland. Because shippers and captains protested, the station continued operating. Five years later the light and fog signal were automated and the resident keepers left, but Coast Guard personnel from La Push returned to the island regularly.

DOROTHY ZAUNER ARMSTRONG

Christian Zauner, shown near retirement, was Destruction Island's first keeper.

During 1970 and 1971, coast guardsman Gary Lentz made many trips to the station by helicopter. He remembers nights alone on the island when the light's twenty-four beams circled through the fog. "It was like looking up into a carnival ride," he said.

In those days, the automatic sensors and monitoring equipment were not reliable. "When we left the island we'd just turn the fog signal on to run continuously," Lentz said. "We'd often drive down the highway from La Push to look across the water to be sure everything was in order."

By then the old fog signal and its coal-fired boilers had long since been replaced by a modern, diesel-operated fog signal. Part of the old fog signal building had been converted into temporary living quarters. The original principal keepers' dwelling had been burned, and Lentz was assigned the task of burning the assistant keepers' dwelling.

127

Where the old lamp had been, a halogen bulb burned, with banks of batteries at the ready in case shore power failed. But, like earlier keepers, Lentz still had to clean the lens and polish its brass. One sunny day, while standing inside the lens to clean it, he smelled something burning. The sun's rays, focused by the lens, had ignited a cleaning rag. Lentz quickly put the fire out, then drew the lantern room curtains around the lens.

In 1995, the original lens was removed and replaced by a modern optic. For coast guardsman Jim Dillon, who was there to assist, it was a special time. In a ceremony held before removal began, Dillon stood inside the lens and was sworn in for reenlistment.

Disassembly took about a week. Each section of the lens was wrapped in bubble wrap and foam, then crated up. The crates, once lowered to the ground, filled one truck-size container that was airlifted to Port Angeles, then shipped to Tongue Point, Oregon, for storage. In 1998 the lens was placed on permanent display at the Westport Maritime Museum in Westport.

Today personnel of the Coast Guard Aids to Navigation Team Astoria, Oregon, come to the Destruction Island station by helicopter once every three months. Solar panels charge the batteries to power the light and electric fog signal. When the men stay overnight, they use the cramped quarters in the original fog signal building where the silent trumpets are still in place.

Direction and Hours

The island is closed to the public. However, the lighthouse can be seen from US 101 at a viewpoint about a mile south of Ruby Beach.

To see the station's first-order Fresnel lens, visit the Westport Maritime Museum at 2201 West Haven Drive in Westport. It's open daily, Memorial Day weekend through Labor Day, 10-5. The rest of the year, Wed. to Fri., 12-4; Sat. and Sun., 10-5. Phone (360) 268-0078.

26. Cape Flattery Lighthouse

The Cape Flattery Lighthouse stands on Tatoosh Island, the most northwesterly point of the contiguous United States. The third lighthouse built in what was then Washington Territory, it has been guiding ships entering and leaving the Strait of Juan de Fuca since 1857.

The island, covering nearly twenty acres, is about a mile northwest of Cape Flattery. Dangerous shoals and rocks extend beyond the island's steep cliffs, and a small beach lies on the north side.

For centuries Makah Indians spent summers on the island, living in cedar-plank houses built on rocks above the beach. From the plateau they watched for whales. In 1788 fur trader John Meares named the island for Makah chief Tatooche.

The United States Coast Survey began its search for lighthouse sites on the West Coast in 1849, and Tatoosh Island was one of those selected. One survey member reported, "to vessels bound from seaward a lighthouse on this island would be of much assistance. It would enable them to enter the Straits, when the absence of a light would frequently compel them to remain at sea until daylight."

Though funds were appropriated for a lighthouse at Cape Flattery by 1855, the Lighthouse Board reported that work at Tatoosh Island had been delayed "on account of Indian war." At the time, uprisings were occurring in Washington Territory over treaties signed earlier.

When construction did begin on the island, the first structure built was a blockhouse where the workers lived. Contractor Isaac Smith also issued twenty muskets, but they were never fired.

Materials were landed on the beach and lifted by derrick to the plateau. Sandstone blocks two feet thick were used for the base of the lighthouse, a Cape Cod–style dwelling with a sixty-five-foot tower rising from the center. Except for the height of its tower, the lighthouse was a mirror image of the one being built at New Dungeness at the same time. Two weeks after the New Dungeness light was lit, Cape Flattery displayed its light from a first-order Fresnel lens on December 28, 1857.

George Gerrish, the first principal keeper, and three assistants moved into the new lighthouse, but soon found they had little to celebrate. Inferior whale oil clogged the wicks, making it difficult to keep the light properly lit. The men soon became weary of the isolation and low pay, and Gerrish and two of the assistants resigned after three months.

The collector of customs, who was in charge of aids to navigation in the district, hastily assigned Franklin Tucker and two other men. Tucker had just finished as temporary keeper at New Dungeness. These men, too, resigned after three months, blaming the low pay and their fear of the Makahs, who still used the island.

In 1860 William W. Winsor became the principal keeper. His friend James Swan came for a short visit, but storms and wind delayed his departure for two weeks. Swan enjoyed the company of the lighthouse keepers, all former ships' captains, but he found the dwelling uncomfortable. Moss grew on the interior walls, rain seeped under the shingles, and wind blowing across the chimney filled the rooms with smoke.

Winsor was replaced by George K. Smith in 1862. The lighthouse inspector questioned the assignment, because George had been appointed by his son, Victor Smith, the new collector of customs for the Puget Sound district.

The inspector reported, "The light is in deplorable condition. He [George Smith] has with him two assistants who are as ignorant as he is. They have got the light out of order and are unable to repair it." In the same report, the inspector recommended that a family occupy the lighthouse, so it would be "no longer at the mercy of the

The Cape Flattery Lighthouse on Tatoosh Island, the most northwesterly point in the contiguous United States, circa 1880.

rollicking bachelors who have had possession since its establishment."

Three years later George Smith left Cape Flattery for a new assignment. His son Victor had appointed him the first principal keeper of the Ediz Hook Lighthouse.

In 1872 the fog bell originally installed near the tower was replaced by a steam whistle. About the same time, the Lighthouse Board recognized the unsatisfactory condition of the keepers' quarters. The board wanted to provide a comfortable dwelling that "would enable a better class of keepers to be retained here than would be willing to occupy the present dwelling." A new dwelling was completed in 1875, and the old one was repaired.

Like the early keepers, J. C. Floyd, who was the principal keeper in the late 1870s, was concerned about keeping the lamp lit. Floyd wrote the collector of customs that he had only a few days' oil supply left. Fearing the light would be extinguished, the collector chartered a schooner and sent it to Victoria, British Columbia. There the captain picked up 110 gallons of whale oil and delivered it to Neah Bay, a Makah village, seven miles east of Tatoosh. Makahs were hired to transport the oil to the island in their dugouts, and the oil arrived in time.

Except for supplies lightered ashore from the lighthouse tender, deliveries of mail, firewood, people, even cows and a piano arrived by dugout. These were loaded at Neah Bay and paddled by Makahs with nicknames such as "Lighthouse Jack" and "Old Doctor," through the waves to the island's beach.

The first keeper to bring his family to Tatoosh was Captain Henry Ayers. A Union officer during the Civil War, Ayers brought his wife and his young daughter, Jesse, with him when in 1885 he was assigned to assist principal keeper Alex Sampson.

Sampson was a favorite among the Makahs, the other lightkeepers, and children who visited the island. He was described as "a big man, slightly stooped, with iron gray hair and beard, and the weathered face of a man who has spent a lifetime at sea." Sampson had earned his weathered look. Born into a Massachusetts shipping family, he had served as the master of several large vessels. In the 1850s he built a house on the future site of Port Angeles and retained his home while he was a keeper.

Sampson's knowledge of ships and navigation proved valuable. One afternoon after many fog-shrouded days accompanied by the incessant blowing of the steam fog signal, the fog began to lift. Suddenly, a three-masted square-rigger with all sails set appeared in the reef-filled channel between the island and the mainland. Sampson grabbed his "speaking horn" and ran to the island's edge. Shouting directions through the horn and waving his arm, he showed the captain where the deepest channel lay. The captain corrected his course, and dipped his flag as he sailed safely past the island. Sampson retired from Cape Flattery and lightkeeping in 1893.

Winters were often dreary on Tatoosh. Storms hammered the island with strong winds and heavy rains. Though the lighthouse

COAST GUARD MUSEUM NORTHWEST

A Makah Indian summer encampment on Tatoosh Island, circa 1880.

was built of sandstone and brick, the tower vibrated in high winds, "in a manner calculated to terrify a person of weak nerves," wrote one keeper. During these howling storms, keepers were required to stay in the lantern room all night to keep the lamp burning. Some assistant keepers resigned rather than stand watch in the swaying tower.

Still, others felt pride in their work, like the keeper who wrote in the log during the 1880s:

"And on dark, stormy nights when far at sea,
This beacon bursts upon the mariners' sight.
They shape their course, from doubt and danger free,
And bless the keepers of Cape Flattery Light."

In 1883 the United States Signal Corps built a weather station on Tatoosh. The wooden buildings were lashed to rocks to keep them from blowing away.

Frank Beahan was on the weather station's original staff. He

133

married two years later and brought his bride to live on the island, where their daughters, Hazel and Ruth, were born. When Hazel was eleven, she and Ruth happily watched the number of children on the island suddenly increase with the arrival of new principal keeper John M. Cowan.

Cowan, his wife, and their seven children landed on the island in May 1900. He had joined the Lighthouse Service in 1893, and had previously served at Oregon's Heceta Head and Coquille River lighthouses.

Later, in an interview for a newspaper article, Hazel Beahan reminisced about playing with the Cowan children. "In those days juvenile delinquency consisted of lowering a companion down the cliffs on a rope to rob gulls' nests" and struggling to pull the friend up before being discovered by their parents.

At the end of summer, the pranks ended when the Cowan children left to live with relatives in Portland, Oregon, where they attended school. About ten years later, John Cowan's eldest son, Forrest, became one of his assistant keepers.

On a Saturday in February 1911, Forrest and four others, including a newlywed couple, decided to attend a dance in Neah Bay. The weather was mild but the seas were rough, and the group was advised not to make the trip. Nevertheless, they launched a boat from the beach. Going through the surf, the boat capsized and was pulled from the shore by a strong ebb tide. The elder Cowan saw the young people clinging to the boat's sides. He launched the station boat and saved two of the men, but his son and the others were lost.

Gale force winds struck the Oregon and Washington coasts in January 1921. Mrs. Cowan later wrote that the winds "blew Mr. Cowan end over end for 300 feet. Only by clinging to the grass and crawling on his hands and knees was he able to avoid being blown from the island into the sea." A bull from the Tatoosh herd was blown off the island, and in the lighthouse log he was described as lost at sea. But the bull surprised everyone by swimming to shore. He was rewarded with extra rations.

Around the time that Cowan retired in 1932, the first-order lens was replaced by a fourth-order Fresnel lens. Cowan was seventy and had been with the Lighthouse Service for thirty-nine years. His proudest boast was that during his time at Tatoosh, the light never failed. He and Mrs. Cowan moved to a six-acre farm east of Port Angeles, where he died two years later.

At one time during the 1930s about forty people lived on Tatoosh Island to operate the lighthouse, the weather station, and a United States Navy radio compass station. The small community had a post office and schoolhouse where seventeen children attended classes.

Even more people moved to the island during World War II. Navy personnel arrived to staff a Navy decoding station, and a detachment of marines was assigned to protect it and island residents.

After the war, the island population dwindled. First the Navy and the marines left. In the 1950s about twenty residents remained; in 1966 the weather station and its buildings were demolished. Coast Guard keepers left after the light and a modern fog signal were automated in 1977. A modern optic lens has replaced the fourth-order lens. Yet today, as on the day the light was first lit, the lighthouse still stands.

Directions and Hours

Tatoosh Island is closed to the public. However, the lighthouse may be seen via a thirty-minute walk to a viewpoint on Cape Flattery. The trailhead is at a parking area about eight miles west of Neah Bay off SR 112.

The lighthouse tender *Shubrick*, a sidewheel steamer built in 1857, was the West Coast's first Lighthouse Service vessel.

SHIPS AND SIGNALS

Two kinds of ships played important roles in guiding mariners along Washington's coast and its inland waters.

Lightships served as floating lighthouses, marking wave-swept shoals, dangerous reefs, or major waterway entrances. The ships were held in position by long chains attached to mushroom-shaped anchors. Each lightship had a unique light and sound characteristic so mariners could identify it at night or in thick fog.

Lighthouse tenders were the lifelines of the early lighthouses, which were usually in such remote locations that the materials for building them had to be delivered by ship. Once the lighthouse stations were established, the tenders supplied and serviced them, as well as bringing long-awaited relief crews to the lightships.

Signals of light and sound, also unique to each lighthouse station, guided mariners along Washington's shores in darkness, fogs, and storms.

The Fresnel lens, starting in 1822, became the epitome of efforts to signal mariners with light — efforts that began around 300 B.C., when a wood fire was lit atop an Egyptian tower on the island of Pharos.

Bells produced the first signals of sound at Washington's lighthouse stations. It wasn't until the 1870s that more efficient devices began to be used to guide mariners.

27. Lightships

Three lightship stations served mariners along Washington's coast: one at the entrance to the Columbia River, one marking a dangerous reef off Cape Alava, and one near the entrance to the Strait of Juan de Fuca. Nearly a dozen different vessels were employed at these three locations between 1892 and 1979. Each vessel and station developed its own unique history and character.

The lightships were 100 to 150 feet in length, with beams up to thirty feet. Mushroom-shaped anchors, with anchor chains weighing nearly fifteen tons and up to 1,300 feet long, held the ships in position.

Each ship had a forward pilothouse with a superstructure behind. Its hull was painted in distinguishing colors, and the name of its station was painted in bold letters on the vessel's sides. Most of the ships had two masts from which the lights were displayed. They also had fog signals and, later, submarine bells that transmitted sound through the water and radio beacons that sent distinctive electronic signals.

The first lightship off Washington was also the first on the West Coast. It was stationed eight miles southwest of Cape Disappointment, near the Columbia River's entrance. During this period, lightships were numbered in the order in which they were built, and Light Vessel *No. 50* was the first one assigned to the Columbia River station.

This wooden vessel, built in San Francisco, had no engine, but carried sails for emergencies. It was towed to its station in April 1892. Two coal-fired boilers produced steam for the fog signal. Six large lamps on each mast cast light in all directions. Round screens

The Swiftsure Lightship Station, northwest of Cape Flattery, was the last of three stations established off Washington's coast.

mounted atop the masts made the lightship more recognizable in daytime.

In November 1899, *No. 50*'s anchor chain parted during a gale, and though the sails were raised, the ship blew shoreward during the night. At dawn, two tugs and the lighthouse tender *Manzanita* arrived to help. Just when rescue seemed within reach, a towline snapped, and further efforts to save the ship proved futile. The ship went aground on the ocean beach near Cape Disappointment, but the captain and seven crewmen were saved.

Repeated efforts to pull the ship off the sand were unsuccessful. After sixteen months, a Portland house-moving firm placed rollers under the vessel and, using horses and winches, began to haul the ship 700 yards across a peninsula to the shore of Baker Bay on the Columbia River.

On June 2, 1901, *No. 50* was launched into the bay. It was repaired in Portland, then towed back to its station.

Umatilla Reef was the location of the second Washington lightship. This reef is about two miles offshore at the western end of a jumble of sea stacks, islets, and rocks that extend from Cape Alava, about twenty miles south of Cape Flattery. An early *Coast Pilot* described the reef as "in some respects . . . the greatest danger on the northern coast. Because it is a very difficult object to make out."

Johnny "Dynamite" O'Brien could attest to the danger. In February 1884, he was the first officer on the steamer *Umatilla* as it thrashed about in high seas and blinding snow before grounding on the reef. The crew abandoned ship, but after the storm abated, O'Brien and two crewmen returned in a raft. The ship had worked free, so they raised the headsails and cleared the reef. The *Umatilla* was towed away and later returned to service, and the reef was given the ship's name.

Fifteen years later, in May 1898, Light Vessel *No. 67* was positioned near the dangerous reef. The ship was propelled by a steam engine and equipped with a twelve-inch steam whistle, oil lamps at the mastheads, and a submarine bell. The clanging of the submerged bell could be heard fifteen miles away by ships equipped with a listening device.

Washington's third lightship station was established in 1909 on the Swiftsure Bank. About fifteen miles northwest of Cape Flattery, it marked the entrance to the Strait of Juan de Fuca. The first vessel to serve at this station was Light Vessel *No. 93*, its steel hull painted yellow to distinguish it from the nearby Umatilla lightship. It steamed under its own power, carrying emergency sails and the same equipment as *No. 67*.

Each lightship needed periodic maintenance and overhaul, requiring it to be off station for about three months in a typical year. Also, the ships often had to return to port for repairs after being damaged in storms.

COLUMBIA RIVER MARITIME MUSEUM

After grounding on an ocean beach, Columbia River lightship *No. 50* was salvaged by a Portland house-moving firm.

As early as 1898, the Lighthouse Board sought appropriations for a relief lightship to temporarily replace the assigned vessels along the Pacific coast. The board's request was finally answered in 1905, when Light Vessel *No. 76* began relieving the other vessels; it was replaced by *No. 92* in 1909. Relief vessels were red, with "Relief" painted on their sides. Their light and fog signal characteristics could be adjusted to match those of the lightship being relieved.

In 1909, the first lightship, *No. 50*, was retired and was replaced by *No. 88*, a steam-powered, steel-hulled vessel. Built on the East Coast, *No. 88* came around Cape Horn with other Lighthouse Service vessels to take up its station near the Columbia River's entrance.

In the stormy early morning darkness of January 13, 1913, the tanker *Rosecrans*, carrying twenty thousand barrels of crude oil, steamed by the lightship searching for the river's bar. The tanker ran aground north of the entrance. Near dawn the lifesaving station at Cape Disappointment heard the captain's distress call on the wireless.

By mid-morning a lifeboat crossed the foaming bar and reached the wrecked tanker. The lifesaving crew found four men clinging to the rigging above the breakers. One leaped into the water and died before he could be pulled to the lifeboat, but the others were saved. Since it was impossible for the lifeboat to return across the treacherous bar, the only refuge was the lightship. With great difficulty, the survivors and lifeboat crew were hauled aboard. They remained on the lightship for several days until the winds calmed and they could return to shore.

Life aboard a lightship was not usually so exciting. For endless days and nights, as the lightship lay at the end of its anchor chain in the fog, the crew could often do nothing but listen as unseen ships churned by. On the East Coast, collisions with lightships were frequent; in 1919, one was cut in half and sunk by a vessel lost in the fog. Luckily, none of Washington's lightships met this fate.

The essence of lightship life was captured by Archie Binns in his 1934 novel, *Lightship*. Binns served on a lightship at Umatilla Reef, and described a night on the fog-enshrouded vessel. He wrote, "Nothing was left in the world except the ship, rolling its lights aloft mistily, beating out its number on the sea-muffled bell and racked at two-minute intervals with the spasm of its whistle, like the recurring pain in some monstrous travail. Below there was the clash of a shovel on the floor plates of the fire room."

Lightships were usually manned by twelve to sixteen men. In the early days, the crews remained on the vessel for ninety days, followed by thirty days ashore. After 1939, each lightship had a crew of twenty-one men, fourteen on duty and seven on shore leave. The men spent two weeks aboard and one week ashore.

Officers were hard pressed to keep the isolated crews busy.

On-duty hours were spent in endless chores of cleaning and painting. Off-duty time was devoted to hobbies, reading, and knot tying. Chess and the card game acey-deucey were popular pastimes. Fishing lines were almost always over the side, yielding abundant catches of salmon, halibut, and cod. Many ship's cooks were adept at canning, and crewmembers frequently brought canned fish home to their friends and families.

The crews also sought the camaraderie of others at sea. Fishermen were friendly and talkative, and often willing to bring personal items from shore to the lightship crew.

More distant but important relationships were built with other vessels. On December 25, 1917, the crew of the Umatilla lightship watched the liner *Queen* approach the reef. The ship slowed and the skipper shouted an order to his boatswain. Two large boxes fell into the water and were quickly retrieved by the lightship crew. They were delighted to discover that the boxes contained fresh meat, fruit, and vegetables for their Christmas dinner.

Commercial radio and later television helped break the monotony. In the early years of radio, the receivers interfered with the ships' own radio equipment, so their use was limited. When television came, crews sometimes would switch channels until they found a weather reporter whose forecast would assure them that their relief crews would arrive on schedule.

World War II brought temporary changes to Washington's lightship fleet. The Umatilla lightship, *No. 88*, and the Swiftsure lightship, *No. 113*, were temporarily replaced by lighted whistle buoys so they could be assigned to the U.S. Navy. The lightships were painted gray and fitted with radar and deck-mounted guns, and their quarters were enlarged to accommodate thirty-four men. *No. 88* tracked inbound vessels off the Strait of Juan de Fuca, and *No. 113* performed similar duties in Alaska.

The Columbia River lightship remained on station during the war and came close to hostile fire. In 1942 a Japanese submarine shelled the coast near the mouth of the Columbia. The ship's lights were extinguished, for its crew did not want to meet the same fate as the Diamond Shoals lightship off North Carolina, which had been sunk by a German submarine during World War I.

The coming of electronically automated aids to navigation heralded the end of the lightship fleet. In 1961, the Umatilla lightship was replaced by an automated buoy. After a few months the buoy proved to be inadequate, so the Swiftsure lightship *No. 113* was repainted with "Umatilla" on its sides and moved to the reef. In 1971, however, that ship was permanently replaced by a buoy, leaving only the Columbia River lightship. An automated buoy replaced this last lightship in October 1979, bringing Washington's lightship history to a close.

Private groups and individuals sought to save some of the historic vessels from the scrap yard. It was a bittersweet period. With pennants flying, lightships were taken to what was hoped to be their final port. Newspapers hailed the events with headlines that read, "*No. 88* Home from the Seas Forever," and "Last Glimmer of Hope for Lightship." Later headlines read, "Swift's Light Doomed to the Graveyard," and "No Relief for the Lightship Relief."

For seventeen years *No. 88* was docked at the Columbia River Maritime Museum at Astoria, Oregon. Then a restaurateur in Cathlamet, Washington, purchased it. When his business failed, the ship went to Canadian interests.

The last Swiftsure lightship was brought to Gig Harbor, Washington, but it proved unpopular in that small bay. The vessel was taken to Portland, Oregon, where it sank. Recovered, it served as a floating restaurant at Newport, Oregon. When that venture failed, the old lightship sank again, this time while under tow off Oregon's Cape Lookout on its way to Tacoma, Washington.

Three lightships still survive on the West Coast. Light Vessel *No. 83* is being restored at Seattle, Washington, by Northwest Seaport. Built in 1904, this ship has its original steam engines and is one of the oldest surviving lightships in the country. Depending on the amount of support they receive in the form of donations and volunteers, the sponsors plan to display the vessel regularly on Seattle's Lake Union and at the Swiftsure Banks for the annual Swiftsure sailboat races.

The last Columbia River lightship, *WAL 604*, is in mint condition and can be visited at the Columbia River Maritime Museum in Astoria, Oregon. A third lightship, *WAL 605*, is moored at Oakland, California, where it is being restored by volunteers under the auspices of the U.S. Lighthouse Society.

Directions and Hours

The Columbia River Maritime Museum is in Astoria, Oregon, at 1792 Marine Drive. Open daily 9:30-5 except Thanksgiving and Christmas. Phone (503) 325-2323.

For the status of work on Light Vessel *No. 83*, call Northwest Seaport at (206) 447-9800. For information about the lightship in Oakland, call the U.S. Lighthouse Society at (415) 362-7255.

28. Lighthouse Tenders

Lighthouse tenders were important in the often lonely lives of the early keepers and their families. On "Boat Day" the tender arrived with flags flying, bringing fuel for the lamps and fog signals, flour, tinned goods, catalogs, mail, and the keepers' pay. And often on board was the lighthouse inspector, who came to examine everything from the cleanliness of the kitchen cupboards to the polish of the lens.

Early tenders were 140 to 200 feet long with sleek lines to enhance speed. They usually had a long foredeck with a hold beneath to carry supplies and building materials. A derrick mounted forward handled heavy cargo. Behind the derrick stood a pilothouse, and a spacious inspector's cabin was near the stern. Cabin space was also available for keepers and their families who were being transferred from station to station. Crewing varied, but usually about twenty men and six officers were on board.

The first lighthouse tender on the West Coast was the sidewheel steamer *Shubrick*. Built in Philadelphia, Pennsylvania, in 1857, it was 140 feet long with a twenty-two-foot beam. In addition to its steam boiler, it had two masts with sails.

When the *Shubrick* was built, there was unrest among Northwest Native Americans, and tribes from Canada were making armed incursions into Puget Sound. Therefore the tender carried one cannon forward and two cannons aft. A hose of copper and leather was connected to the boiler so crews could repel hostile boarders with scalding water. Fortunately, the cannons were never fired in anger, and the hose system went unused.

The *Shubrick*'s adventurous career began with a trip around

Cape Horn to San Francisco in 1858. The ship ran out of fuel in the Strait of Magellan, and the crew burned the ship's furniture and hardwood paneling before reaching a source of wood in Chile. After it arrived at its home port at the Lighthouse Service depot in San Francisco, one of the ship's first assignments was to set the buoys marking the channel at the Columbia River's entrance.

During the Civil War, the *Shubrick* was assigned to the U.S. Revenue Service. While serving as a revenue cutter in Washington waters, it trained its loaded guns on the customshouse at Port Townsend in 1862. The town's residents were protesting the taking of the customs records to a new port of entry at Port Angeles. The customs records were removed, and the guns were not fired.

In 1865 the *Shubrick* was assigned to the U.S. Navy under the command of Captain C. M. Scammon. Along with other vessels, it sailed to the Bering Strait to establish a transcontinental cable link through Siberia. That effort was abandoned when a cable was laid to Europe from the U.S. East Coast. However, Captain Scammon learned much about whales on his voyage to the north. When he returned, he wrote and illustrated *Marine Mammals of the North Pacific*. Published in 1874, the book became the standard reference on whales for many years.

The *Shubrick* was reassigned to the Lighthouse Service in 1866. Carrying construction material to Cape Mendocino, California, it ran aground and was nearly abandoned. Like the Columbia River lightship, the *Shubrick* was dragged five hundred yards along the beach. Successfully salvaged, the vessel was repaired and returned to service.

When the *Shubrick* arrived on the West Coast, only fourteen lighthouses were in operation there. Seventeen years later, the *Shubrick* was still the coast's only lighthouse tender, but there were thirty-four lighthouses to service from San Diego Bay to Puget Sound.

The Lighthouse Board stated that this one tender could no longer

In one year, the lighthouse tender *Heather* steamed over 17,000 miles servicing lighthouse stations in the Pacific Northwest.

do all the work necessary. The next year the board stated that "An appropriation for a new vessel would relieve the board from embarrassment." Congress heard the plea and provided funds for a new tender.

The screw steamer *Manzanita* was completed in Baltimore, Maryland, in 1879. It was one of the first in an unbroken line of tenders named for shrubs, trees, or flowers. Arriving on the West Coast, the *Manzanita* was assigned to California's lighthouses. The *Shubrick*'s home port became Tongue Point, Oregon, from which it tended the lights and buoys in Oregon, Washington, and Alaska.

In 1885 the venerable *Shubrick* was scrapped and burned on a mud flat in San Francisco Bay, with only its copper and brass salvaged. The *Manzanita* took its place in Northwest waters and a new tender, the *Madrona,* was home ported at the Yerba Buena depot in San Francisco Bay.

By 1903, the lighthouse tenders *Columbine* and *Heather* had joined the *Manzanita* in the Northwest. In fiscal year 1905, the three vessels steamed nearly 44,000 miles while delivering 894 tons of coal, plus supplies and building materials to light stations from Oregon to Alaska.

The *Manzanita* was rammed and sank on the Columbia River in 1905. A new vessel of the same name, built in 1908, survived its sister ships and served in Washington waters until 1948.

The successors to the lighthouse tenders are Coast Guard buoy tenders. These utilitarian vessels have large booms and open decks to transport and service buoys. Today the buoy tenders *Bayberry* and *Mariposa* are stationed in Seattle and the *Cowslip* sails from Tongue Point, Oregon. Their principal mission is maintaining buoys and other aids to navigation accessible only by water. The vessels are also employed in search and rescue, and in marine pollution control.

New buoy tenders are being built for the Coast Guard. As in the past, some will be named for plants, while others will be named for famous lighthouse keepers.

The first-order Fresnel lens from Destruction Island is on permanent display at the Westport Maritime Museum.

29. Lenses and Lamps, Bells and Whistles

America's first lighthouse was built in 1716 at the entrance to Boston Harbor. By 1853, when work began on the first eight West Coast lighthouses, including Cape Disappointment, nearly 300 lighthouses stood along the nation's eastern shores, the Gulf of Mexico, and the Great Lakes.

The earliest U.S. lighthouses used lamps as lights. In 1812 a system of lamps and parabolic reflectors was adopted. For a time, circular lenses were used in front of the lamps, but the inferior glass actually diminished their brightness.

In 1822 French optician Augustin Fresnel (Fra-NELL) perfected a system of lenses and prisms that focused a lamp's light in a strong horizontal beam. The Fresnel lens consisted of a central lens with tiers of dioptric prisms above and below. These prisms refracted the light and directed it outward. Above and below these elements were catadioptric prisms which captured the oblique rays from the light source and reflected and refracted them so they became a part of the horizontal beam.

Though the Fresnel lens was more powerful than any system previously devised, the U.S. lighthouse bureaucracy did not adopt it until 1852. The system has stood the test of time — today six Washington lighthouses still have an operating Fresnel lens lit by an electric bulb.

Fresnel lenses were made in several sizes, called "orders," based on their inside diameter. First-order lenses were the largest, weighing nearly four tons and measuring six feet in diameter. They stood nearly twelve feet high, and up to seventeen feet with the pedestal mount included. Smaller fourth-order lenses were about twenty inches in diameter and about three feet high.

Larger lenses, with lights that could be seen about twenty miles out to sea, were used along the seacoast. Smaller lenses were used as harbor lights or along inland waters, as their lights could be seen about fifteen miles.

Regardless of its size, each lens was made in sections held together by finely crafted brass frames. The sections were shipped in crates from England or France, and then the lens was reassembled at the lighthouse site by matching numbers engraved in the frames.

To enable mariners to distinguish one light from another, the light at each lighthouse had a distinctive characteristic. A fixed light was produced by a drum lens. Its central lens was a convex band of glass that extended around the circumference of the lens. Combined with prisms above and below, it cast a fan-shaped beam of light.

Flashing lights were produced by a rotating lens that had anywhere from one to twenty-four panels. Each panel, with a central bullseye lens and prisms above and below, cast a concentrated pencil-beam of light. The lens was mounted on ball bearings or chariot wheels, or floated in a bed of mercury. It was rotated first by a hand-wound clockwork mechanism, later by electric motor. The light's characteristic was produced by varying the number of lighted and blank panels, the rotation speed, and the use of colored screens.

The lens and lamp were mounted atop the tower inside a metal-framed glass enclosure, called the lantern, which protected them from the weather. Vents in the metal wall beneath the glass could be adjusted to supply air to the flame, to keep condensation off the windows, and to remove fumes from the lamp. Air escaped through a vent in the lantern's roof.

The lamps first used with the Fresnel lens had from two to five wicks. These wicks were hollow, allowing oxygen to flow both around and within them to produce a bright flame.

Many different fuels were used in the lamps. Whale oil was preferred until its price reached $2.50 per gallon, too expensive for

Cleaning the Fresnel lens was a daily chore for early keepers.

lights like Cape Disappointment that consumed 170 gallons per month. Other fuels were tested, including rapeseed oil, olive oil, and porpoise oil. Lard oil was adopted in the 1860s, and by the 1880s it was replaced by kerosene.

The soot produced by the oil lamps was the bane of early lighthouse keepers' existence. An 1861 bulletin to keepers stated, "Unless the illuminating apparatus, lamps, and lantern glass of the lighthouse are kept clean and in good condition, a good light cannot be produced, and mariners will complain." A keeper's first morning chore was cleaning the night's accumulation of soot off the lens, lamps, and lantern.

In 1908 the incandescent oil vapor lamp (IOV) came into use, giving a six-fold increase in candlepower over the wick lamps. This lamp worked like a Coleman lantern: air pressure forced the kerosene into the lamp, where it was vaporized and burned in a mantle.

This system remained in use until electric lights were introduced.

The efficiency and power of electricity dramatically changed lightkeeping. Many Fresnel lenses have been replaced by modern optics. These small optics with plastic lenses can produce a fixed light or lights that flash by rotation or with electronic flashers. When the bulb fails, it is automatically replaced by another. They can be operated by shore power or by solar-powered batteries.

Yet even the most powerful light is of little use in the fog. The first U.S. fog signal was a cannon fired at intervals from the Boston lighthouse in 1719. Bells were used at several early Washington lighthouses.

By the late 1800s, three new types of fog signal were employed. Steam whistles, like those used on locomotives, were adapted for lighthouse use. Sirens produced sound by sending steam through a slotted, fixed plate and a rotating disk. Daboll fog signals used compressed air or steam to vibrate a reed in a resonating cavity. The latter two systems used trumpets to resonate and direct the sound. At first these systems used prodigious amounts of coal or wood. In the early 1900s, oil-fired burners were introduced.

Today's fog signals are electric, using shore power or solar-powered batteries. They are activated by a microprocessor that measures the amount of fog in the atmosphere.

Lights and fog signals are no longer essential to mariners with modern electronic equipment. A vessel's position can be pinpointed with radar or a Global Positioning System (GPS) tuned to satellite signals. To assist mariners in the Strait of Juan de Fuca, Admiralty Inlet, and Puget Sound, the Coast Guard operates the Puget Sound Vessel Traffic Service. This service uses radar on towers, several of which are located at inland waterway lighthouse stations. The vessels are tracked and directed with two-way radio communications.

Still, for boaters without sophisticated equipment, or in the event that modern equipment fails, lighthouses and fog signals serve their original purpose. And they continue to be reminders of Washington's maritime heritage.

Further Reading

Clifford, Mary Louise and J. Candace Clifford. *Women Who Kept the Lights*. Williamsburg, Virginia: Cypress Communications, 1993.

DeWire, Elinor. *Guardians of the Lights: Stories of U.S. Lighthouse Keepers*. Sarasota, Florida: Pineapple Press, Inc., 1995.

Gibbs, Jim. *Twilight on the Lighthouses*. Atglen, Pennsylvania: Schiffer Publishing, Ltd., 1996.

Holland, Francis Ross, Jr. *America's Lighthouses*. New York, New York: Dover Publications, Inc., 1972.

Lighthouse Digest. Monthly magazine. Lighthouse Depot, P.O. Box 427, Wells, Maine 04090.

Nelson, Sharlene and Ted Nelson. *Umbrella Guide to California Lighthouses*. Seattle, Washington: Epicenter Press, 1993.

———. *Umbrella Guide to Oregon Lighthouses*. Seattle, Washington: Epicenter Press, 1994.

Roberts, Bruce and Ray Jones. *Pacific Northwest Lighthouses*. Old Saybrook, Connecticut: The Globe Pequot Press, 1997.

Shelton-Roberts, Cheryl and Bruce Roberts. *Lighthouse Families*. Birmingham, Alabama: Crane Hill Publishers, 1997.

The Keepers Log. Quarterly membership journal. U.S. Lighthouse Society, 244 Kearny Street, Fifth Floor, San Francisco, California, 94108. (415) 362-7255.

Lighthouse Summary

Admiralty Head: Chapter 8. Established 1861. Relocated 1903. Decommissioned 1922. Second lighthouse in Fort Casey State Park. Tours.

Alki Point: Chapter 4. Post light 1887-1912. Lighthouse established 1913. Modern optic. Original Fresnel lens displayed at Admiralty Head. Tours.

Browns Point: Chapter 6. Post light 1887-1902. First tower 1903. Second tower 1933. Modern optic. Leased to Tacoma Metropolitan Parks District. Points Northeast Historical Society custodian. Tours and lodging.

Burrows Island: Chapter 15. Established 1906. Modern optic. Closed to the public.

Cape Disappointment: Chapter 21. Established 1856. Fresnel lens. Grounds only accessible, pending transfer to Washington State Parks. Original Fresnel lens in Lewis and Clark Interpretive Center, Fort Canby State Park.

Cape Flattery (Tatoosh Island): Chapter 26. Established 1857. Modern optic. View from Cape Flattery trail west of Neah Bay.

Cattle Point: Chapter 11. Post light 1888-1934. Tower with fog signal and optic established 1935. Grounds accessible by trail.

Destruction Island: Chapter 25. Established 1892. Modern optic. Original Fresnel lens displayed at the Westport Maritime Museum, Westport. View island from U.S. 101 near Ruby Beach.

Dofflemyer Point: Chapter 7. Post light 1887-1932. Small tower with optic and fog signal established 1933-1934. View from near Boston Harbor.

Ediz Hook: Chapter 19. First lighthouse 1865. Second lighthouse 1908. Decommissioned 1946. Replaced by modern optic at Coast Guard air station.

Grays Harbor: Chapter 24. Established 1898. Modern optic. Original Fresnel lens in tower. Leased to Westport–South Beach Historical Society. Tours.

Lime Kiln: Chapter 12. Established 1914. Present lighthouse established 1919. Modern optic. View from Whale Watch Park in Lime Kiln State Park.

Marrowstone Point: Chapter 10. Post light 1888-1895. Fog signal added 1896. View from beach near Fort Flagler State Park.

Mukilteo: Chapter 1. Established 1906. Fresnel lens. Leased to City of Mukilteo. Mukilteo Historical Society custodians. Tours. Lodging pending completion of dwelling restoration.

New Dungeness: Chapter 17. Established 1857. Modern optic. Second Fresnel lens at Coast Guard Museum Northwest, Seattle. Leased to U.S. Lighthouse Society New Dungeness Chapter. Tours and lodging.

North Head: Chapter 22. Established 1898. Modern optic. Original Fresnel lens at Lewis and Clark Interpretive Center. Tours and lodging. Fort Canby State Park.

Patos Island: Chapter 14. Established 1893. Modern optic. Grounds accessible by boat.

Point No Point: Chapter 2. Established 1880. Fresnel lens. Tours pending lease with Kitsap County Fair and Parks Department.

Point Robinson: Chapter 5. Fog signal 1885. Post light added 1887. Lighthouse established 1915. Leased to Vashon Parks District.

Point Wilson: Chapter 9. Established 1879. Fresnel lens in 1914 tower. Tours pending transfer to Fort Worden State Park.

Semiahmoo: Chapter 16. Established 1905. Decommissioned 1944. Nothing remains. Fresnel lens is privately owned.

Slip Point: Chapter 20. Established 1905. Dismantled 1950s.

Smith Island: Chapter 18. Established 1858. Modern optic on steel tower. Original lighthouse being lost to bluff erosion.

Turn Point: Chapter 13. Established 1893. Small tower with modern optic and fog signal. View by boat or by trail from Reid or Prevost Harbors on Stuart Island.

West Point: Chapter 3. Established 1881. Fresnel lens. View from beach. Discovery Park, Seattle.

Willapa Bay: Chapter 23. Established 1858. Lost to erosion in 1940. Replaced by modern optic on steel tower.

Index

About the Authors

Sharlene and Ted Nelson have been writing about regional history for over forty years. After graduating from the University of California, Berkeley, the couple lived in a northern California logging camp, where Ted was the resident forester. While there, they developed an interest in regional history.

Since then, they have lived in North Carolina, Oregon, and Washington. In each place they chronicled local history in articles, travel magazines, and historical society publications.

While living along the lower Columbia River, they wrote their first book, *Cruising the Columbia and Snake Rivers*, published in 1981. The success of the first edition of *Umbrella Guide to Washington Lighthouses* led to publication of the related *Umbrella Guide to Oregon Lighthouses* and *Umbrella Guide to California Lighthouses*. Their other recent titles include a children's history of logging in the Old West, and children's books about Olympic, Mount Rainier, and Hawaii Volcanos National Parks, and Mount St. Helens National Volcanic Monument, all published by Grolier Publishing Company. Their Epicenter Press book, *Umbrella Guide to Exploring the Columbia-Snake River Inland Waterway*, was published in 1997.

From their Washington home overlooking Puget Sound, Ted and Sharlene sail, ski, and backpack, often with their grandchildren.